ROTTEN GAMBLER TWO
BECOMES A TRUE AMERICAN

ROTTEN GAMBLER TWO BECOMES A TRUE AMERICAN

A Boy's Journey of Surviving the Odds

EDWARD LUMSDAINE

Rotten Gambler Two Becomes a True American:
A Boy's Journey of Surviving the Odds

© 2016 by Edward Lumsdaine
All rights reserved

Printed by CreateSpace, an Amazon.com company
Available from Amazon.com and other retail outlets

Copyright Notes and Sources

The scripture verse is from the HOLY BIBLE, NEW INTERNATIONAL VERSION, copyright ©1973, 1978 and 1984 by the International Bible Society. It is used by permission of Zondervan Bible Publishers.

    The map of China was downloaded from the website www.d-maps.com/carte.php?num_car=3502&lang-en and the Pacific map was from www.d-maps.com/carte.php?num_car=4644&lang-en. This second image was split to form two separate maps. After printing them as a Word document, country and port names as well as the ship's routes were added, before being photographed, followed by cropping and enhancing in Photoshop. These amazing free maps are copyrighted by Daniel Delat.

    The Pacific as a vintage world map was downloaded from http://7-themes.com/6970392-old-world-map-wallpaper.html, then cropped, "stretched," printed, photographed, and enhanced in Photoshop before used as part of the front cover's background.

    The newspaper boy, 3 cents US postage stamp of 1952, is from www.theswedishtiger.com/1015-scotts.html.

    The Chinese words and phrases in the early chapters have been written phonetically exactly as they sound and do not strictly follow the conventions of the pinying system. For example *kung* (as in *kung fu*) sounds like "*goong*"—thus the word for servant is spelled *goong yan*.

For my family

Acknowledgment

I am deeply in debt to Mr. Henning Morgen of A.P. Møller's Records Management Services/Main Archive, Copenhagen, Denmark, for generously sending me a copy of the captain's log of the *Laura Mærsk* for the period I spent on the ship, some photos, the technical drawings and specs of the *Laura Mærsk*, and a book detailing the history of A.P. Møller and the Mærsk Shipping Line—this documentation was crucial for recall and helping me sort out the chronology of my life at sea. He also kindly showed me around the company's headquarters in Copenhagen during a visit in August 2012.

I thank Alison Binks, Dianne Lumsdaine, and Sandra Ashford who read the first draft of the early chapters almost fifteen years ago; their encouragement kept me going.

Also, I very much appreciate the helpful comments by Pastor Alan D. Coker and my son Arnold Lumsdaine who were the first to read and critique an early version of the manuscript completed by 2007. My heartfelt thanks go to Pastor Vern Holstad and Bible Teacher Betty King for their thoughtful review and detailed comments, also in 2007.

I am grateful for the faithful saints (known and unknown) along the path of my life who have kept me in their prayers. God bless you all!

No words can adequately express what I owe my wife for her support, especially during the difficult years and for the labor of love involved in organizing the material, doing the word processing followed by countless rounds of editing and rewrites, and then shaping the final manuscript first into the e-book format for Amazon/Kindle and then this much more exacting softcover version, for which she had to learn how to use Photoshop. She also did the cover design.

While updating the Lumsdaine family tree slideshows for my grandchildren in March 2013, we learned from Milly Ratermann of the existence of *The Grandparent Book* compiled by my sister Yao-tim Lumsdaine in late 1995 (of which Arnold Lumsdaine had a copy). The book helped clarify some information about my parents; it also included the photo of their marriage.

In late October 2015, my wife and I became acquainted with Corrine Sahlberg, former missionary to Thailand. After reading the still incomplete manuscript of my original book entitled *I Bet My Life*, she suggested a change in format that overcame our problem of how to focus my story. She said it was really two books: a "textbook" on how to deal with gambling addiction, and a book for my grandchildren with a focus on love—a point of view also recently suggested by my daughter Anne. From this concept of a split format, we developed the idea of three books—each with a different main focus and organized into shorter chapters. Anne and Corrine—thank you! The three books are:

1. *Rotten Gambler Two Becomes a True American: A Boy's Journey of Surviving the Odds,* © 2016 by Edward Lumsdaine.
2. *Chopsticks and Chocolate: A Love Story betwixt Clashing Cultures* (working title), © 2016 by Edward Lumsdaine and Monika Lumsdaine
3. *Fall and Redemption: A Story of Recovery from Gambling Addiction* (tentative title and time frame), © 2017 by Edward Lumsdaine and Monika Lumsdaine).

All three books will first be formatted as a Kindle e-book, followed by the softcover format printed by CreateSpace. In addition, we are thinking about offering a *Study Guide* with questions and Bible references, with © 2017 by Monika Lumsdaine, to accompany all three books or only Book 3.

Last but not least, I want to express my appreciation to my daughter Anne for painstakingly proof-reading the manuscript several times, with the assistance of her son (whose insight as a hip teenager was helpful and refreshing). What amazed me is how she was able to stir up my memory of childhood events that I had shared with her years ago. Having the eyes, minds and hearts of two younger generations look at my storytelling and making it better is very special to me. Both made many valuable suggestions to improve the clarity of the writing and recommending contemporary words for today's readers.

Above all, my heart overflows with gratitude to God who has patiently watched over me, even when I was determined to go my own way. This book is truly the story of God's love, faithfulness and purpose in the journey of my life, at a time when I did not know Him.

O Lord, you have searched me and you know me.
All the days ordained for me were written in your book
before one of them came to be.
(Psalm 139:1,16, NIV)

Table of Contents

Acknowledgment   vi

Prolog   xi

1 Chop off the Head: Hong Kong and Shanghai   1

2 Life under Japanese Occupation   9

3 Gambit: Early School Years   19

4 Life under the Communists   28

5 Escaping Shanghai   38

6 Hong Kong Interlude: A Way to America   48

7 Life on a Tramp Ship   63

8 Voyage to "New Gold Mountain"   73

9 Getting off at "Old Gold Mountain"   90

10 Encounters in San Francisco   100

11 Military Training   115

12 Ups and Downs in the Philippines   123

13 Ready to Step into the Unknown   135

Epilog   140

About the Author   143

Prolog

I sat in President Shapiro's waiting room at the University of Michigan-Ann Arbor in early 1988, expecting to be called into the conference room for a final interview with the Board of Regents. Since I was one of two finalists for the position of Chancellor of the University of Michigan-Dearborn, I was excited as well as under some stress and in great suspense.

At that time, I had already been Dean of Engineering on the Dearborn campus for five years and had given a campus-wide speech that was very well received. After my presentation, one distinguished faculty member came up to me and said, "I was against you to be our Chancellor, but now I will support you." I left the lecture hall that day feeling I had the backing of not only the engineering faculty and staff, but also my colleagues from the other colleges.

While waiting, my mind drifted back to when I was growing up in Shanghai in one of the poorer sections. I had been expelled from St. Joan of Arc School at age thirteen for playing hooky and fighting, being in Form 1 which is equivalent to grade 6. As I watched my mother cry in front of Brother Gilbert, the headmaster, I was overwhelmed with a desperate longing for America, the country of my father. The Communists had entered Shanghai about two years earlier, in 1949—thus this seemed to be an impossible dream.

This is the story of how I, as a biracial child, penniless, with little formal education, hardly speaking English, and without a clue of how to go about it, got to America, pursued the American dream, and became a true American. By the way, I did not become chancellor, but that is a tale to be told elsewhere.

I have tried to be as accurate as possible in recounting the events of my early life. When in doubt, I have checked facts with my siblings, cousins, and additional sources. I have on occasion been astonished when others have perceived a certain situation quite differently than I did from my own perspective, but my goal has been to share *my* memories (and feelings) as truthfully as possible. If mistakes have slipped in, I apologize—I realize my own fallibility due to my young age at one end and my senior lapses at the other end. Thus I ask for mercy, not judgment. However, I thought it wise to change a few names, details, and some events where I felt identification could cause embarrassment to individuals or their families.

My hope is that many readers will find the setting and glimpse of history from 1937 to 1958 focused on China and the US interesting.

1
Chop off the Head: Hong Kong and Shanghai

"*Sah toh* (Chop off the head)!" I knelt on the dirty floor, with a thug shrieking the threat and his accomplice holding a huge knife to my neck. How did I get into this predicament?

At nine years old, I lived in Shanghai and had a large gambling debt (relative to my non-existent income). When I could not pay it, I was beaten. I could either find a way to earn money or steal it. I talked over my plight with my good friend Yu-Min who lived upstairs in our apartment building. His father worked for a bank.

Yu-Min confided, "My father has a lot of shirts we could sell. They are Arrow shirts, many of them new."

"Do you mean we steal these shirts?" I queried.

He explained, "No—we just 'borrow' them, sell them, and then buy back the same shirts later when we have the money."

I looked at him doubtfully. To calm my misgivings, he added, "My father has so many shirts, he will never miss them. Besides, he will be gone for several months to set up a bank in Nanjing and in another northern city."

That seemed like a good plan until I asked, "How are we going to get the money to buy back the shirts?"

Looking for opportunity, I noticed two husky teenage hooligans selling tickets across the street at the theatre where the Japanese during their occupation had placed an *ack-ack* gun. I later learned this was called "scalping." The theatre was always packed, and tickets sold out quickly. The scalpers would stand in line early and buy a stack of tickets, then sell them at an inflated price shortly before the show started.

I asked Yu-Min to fetch the shirts to get me the venture capital I needed. He did, and we sold a stack of shirts to an elderly, bald man who ran a clothing store on Bubbling Well Road East. He said very little and did not ask where we got the shirts. With an occasional *hmm* and constant rotation and click-clack of two walnuts in one hand, he counted out and then gave us the money.

Yu-Min told me I had to sell the tickets in the street alone, as he didn't want to risk being seen by his family. After I bought the tickets the first day, I would walk away every time I saw one of the hooligans. I reinvested the first day's proceeds and bought another stack of tickets the next day, after giving Yu-Min some pocket change.

Just as I completed my second scalping transaction and turned around, one of the thugs grabbed me by the arm and squeezed so hard I thought my arm would fall off. He pulled me aside, and pointing at me with his index finger he said, *"Boo doong* (don't move)." He yanked the rest of the movie tickets from my hand and sold them while I waited on that spot under the watchful eye of his accomplice. Both spoke mainly Shanghai dialect, with some Mandarin mixed in.

After an hour or so—it seemed like a day—they grabbed me and took me to a dingy room in an apartment. One of them drew out a long knife that to me looked like a Samurai sword. He bore down on me and commanded, "Kneel!"

Numb with fear that he was going to behead me, I instantly obeyed. He put the blade to the back of my neck and ordered, "Hand over your money!"

Chop off the Head: Hong Kong and Shanghai

I emptied my pockets while begging, "Don't hurt me."

The other thug kept repeating, *"Sah toh, sah toh."*

The knife wielder then grabbed me by the neck—he was the bigger of the two—and punched me in the face. As I keeled over, I heard him threaten, "If we ever catch you muscling in on our territory again, we really will cut off your head."

To me, this was no idle threat. When I was six years old, one of my cousins graphically described beheadings he had witnessed, where a Japanese soldier with a large sword killed several Chinese accused of being spies. The soldier would bang the back of the prisoner to straighten the neck before chopping off the head. This nightmarish image has stayed with me to this day.

If I had reported the hooligans who had robbed me to the police (if police could be found at all), I would have been ignored. There were numerous gangs of thugs roaming the streets—it was a time of lawlessness. If they had carried out their threat and murdered me, there were simply no resources for an investigation. Too many people were dying and children disappearing without a trace.

My Cantonese mother was fond of quoting the axiom, *"Tsut soi ding tsut sup."* Loosely translated, it says, "Whoever you are at seven, that you will be until seventy." Since most Chinese in those days died before reaching seventy, this saying basically indicated a predestined life pattern or self-fulfilling prophesy. My mother occasionally called me *"larn doe yee,"* which means "rotten gambler two." The number two son—the second male in birth order, which I am—is sometimes seen in China as the family's gambler.

I was born in Shum Shui Po, Kowloon, Hong Kong in

1937. My father had moved his family south from Shanghai to Hong Kong in 1933 after his father's import-export business failed. In those days, the free port of Hong Kong was a British Crown Colony that was booming with entrepreneurs despite the global depression. The city was overrun with cheap laborers from northeastern China who had fled south because of the Japanese invasion of Manchuria in 1931. My father readily found work as a bookkeeper, clerk or secretary. For example, I found a note stating that in 1935, he worked as a secretary for Paramount Studios.

The photo shows my mother holding me (at six months old), with my brother Charlie and sister Yao-tim. My sister Anne died when she was seven months old, shortly before Yao-tim was born. Her Chinese name means "have sweetness."

When I was about two, my parents decided to move back to Shanghai because of the increasing threat of an all-out attack on Hong Kong by the Japanese. Although the Japanese had invaded Shanghai in August 1937, the International Settlement had remained an island of neutrality with business as usual. Roughly 10,000 American and British citizens lived there and were protected by 1,000 US marines.

Since the Japanese had destroyed the rail line from Hong Kong into Mainland China, we had to travel by ship, a journey that entailed serious risks. One of my mother's two brothers and his entire family left first—except one daughter, Ho Siu Hwa, who stayed with us to help my mother care for the children, including May born in 1938. I was told that I was sick, hence the delay in our family's departure.

The ship with our relatives was torpedoed by the Japanese. Hundreds of people died, with only a few survivors, one of them the 14-year old son of one of my mother's cousins who was an excellent swimmer. He clung to a piece of wooden wreckage and was picked up by a Japanese patrol boat. The Japanese were so astonished that he survived that they did not kill him but instead ordered him not to say anything about the sinking of the ship, because killing that many civilians by mistake was not good publicity. This cousin later taught me to swim in Shanghai. He is over ninety today and still lives in Shanghai. Sadly, my little sister May died in Shanghai in 1939.

My father had been called to China in 1929 to help in his father's import-export company. When it went out of business, his father left for Australia, where he was born in 1882 and still had family. My father fit right into the Chinese culture. He was honest and inscrutable, and these character traits were cherished by the Chinese. In 1932, he wed my mother Ho Miao Ying by marriage contract in a simple ceremony performed by a Buddhist monk. This was at a time when marriage was taboo to a *bak guay* (white ghost)—or, as Caucasians were also dubbed, a *guay tzu* (ghost). Beyond the cultural difference, they were far apart in religious belief, my father being a Christian and my mother a Buddhist. Later, my mother would describe their early life as a series of train journeys by my father between Shanghai and Nanjing to escape his father's creditors in the two cities. Neither her father nor his approved of the marriage. His father stopped speaking to him, and her father disinherited her.

My father was addicted to smoking, and my mother joined him when she grew tired of fighting his habit. He eventually died of lung cancer at age 86. But chiefly, I admired him for his courage. Going to China into a strange, turbulent environment with barely a high-school education—some obtained in Australia, some in Seattle, and some in San Francisco at Galileo HS—with only a bit of experience as a clerk and not speaking the language certainly took guts.

My mother who had grown up in a rural area around Canton did not have much schooling. She did not see a need for learning English, so it was my father who had to learn to speak Chinese: Cantonese to communicate with my mother and Mandarin (the common man's version also known as Putonghua) for his work. She would eventually have nine living children to care for in very difficult circumstances, and in later years had to adjust to life in America. There was a hard core to her that enabled her to survive, and she transmitted to her children important Chinese cultural values. For example, it is the children's responsibility to take care of their parents as soon as they are able.

During the summer of 1940, my brother George was born. This was also the year my parents made their marriage "official" at the American Consulate General in Shanghai (shown wearing Western-style garb in the photo below), so that their four children at the time would have US citizenship. According to my sister Yao-tim, the marriage contract signed by a Chinese magistrate in 1932 was not considered legal by the US government.

On the following page is a map of Eastern China. By train, the distance from Shanghai to Hong Kong is 1237 miles. By sea it is 955 nautical miles. Today, with modern aircraft, the distance is 732 miles, taking about 2 hours and 20 minutes.

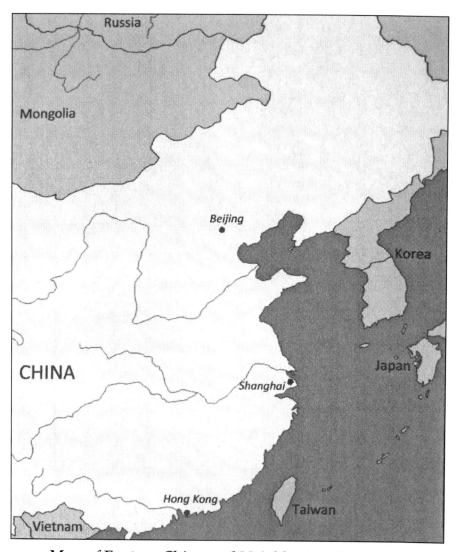

Map of Eastern China and Neighboring Countries

In the next four chapters, I describe my growing up in Shanghai. Life in China was impacted first by Japan's war on China (1937-1945), the rise of Communism, the retreat of the Nationalists to the Island of Taiwan in 1949, and the Korean War (1950-1953), with North Korea supported by Chinese and Soviet Communists and South Korea mainly by the US.

2
Life under Japanese Occupation

The US marines shipped out of Shanghai at the end of November 1941, not having lost a single soldier in the fourteen years they had been in the city. A few days later, the Japanese simultaneously attacked Pearl Harbor, invaded Hong Kong, and also took over the International Settlement in Shanghai.

The Japanese occupied all of Shanghai and unified the city, although they were savage landlords. Shanghai had been carved up before that time because England had beaten China in 1842 in what is known as the First Opium War. That was a disgraceful period in the history of the British Empire because China was forced to take opium in trade for goods, such as spices and silk. After the Second Opium War between China, the British and the French (1856-1860), foreign traders could travel all over China. The previously isolated country had become open to the West. Since then, many countries saw China as an easy mark, and foreigners—English, French, Germans, Italians, and Russians—overran Shanghai and sectioned the city into Concessions, which were areas under the control of the respective countries. We lived in the International Settlement in the center of the city and north of the French Concession.

In this period of white domination, my Australian-born paternal grandfather had gone to China from Seattle to set up an import-export business.

People often ask, "Was your grandfather a missionary?"

To this, my usual answer is, "No, he was a mercenary rather than a missionary, since many foreigners in China at that time exploited the Chinese."

In early 1943, my father, a Caucasian American, was taken by the Japanese to a concentration camp in Pudong across the Huang Pu River from Shanghai. Chinese people were not interned, and my mother could keep her biracial children with her because the oldest was only ten. Had Charlie been sixteen, he would have been interned. We lived on Bubbling Well Road, which is now Nanjing Road West and bisects the city from east to west for most of its length.

When I wrote to an organization called "Old China Hands"—a group of people who survived the Japanese imprisonment in Shanghai and kept records—I received the following information:

> *Your father was interned in the Pudong camp in February 1943. He was listed as being age thirty-seven (in 1945) and a merchant. He was subsequently moved to another camp, the Yu Yuen Road camp. In June 1945 the entire complement of the camp was moved to a complex that was the Japanese military barracks. The purpose of that move was to deter the US Air Force from bombing any barracks once it was known that it contained Allied prisoners.*

During the Japanese occupation, even children came to feel that death was only one misstep away. The mere suspicion of having done something that offended the Japanese in some way could mean death on the spot. They had guard shacks manned by a single soldier every few hundred meters along Bubbling Well Road. We—from toddlers on up—were instructed to bow every time we passed one of these shacks. The Japanese soldiers ruled by absolute terror. The most horrific example—the Rape of Nanking—did not become known in the West until after the end of World War II. Terror was a strategy because there were 100 Chinese civilians for every Japanese soldier.

Here is an incident that happened to me in 1944 when I was seven and still puts a chill down my spine. My mother had asked my brother Charlie to pick up something from a friend's apartment nearby. I always liked to tag along with my oldest brother who was eleven at the time. As we ambled down Bubbling Well Road, we saw three Japanese soldiers marching towards us, one soldier in front, bracketed by the other two slightly behind him. Since the sidewalk was narrow, my brother moved over to the curb. I decided to scoot to the other side to clear the way for the soldiers. I must have been in some panic, thus moved too quickly, stumbled, fell, ricocheted off a wall and hit the leg of the nearest soldier. Terrified and trembling, I got up and bowed quickly, expecting some terrible punishment. However, the soldier simply kicked me aside, like a dog, and kept on walking. I could hardly believe my luck!

By this time, my mother had become a frequent *mahjong* player, and she was exceptionally good at it. Even during the Japanese occupation of Shanghai, my mother would play *mahjong* with friends or relatives. I am not sure, but I believe she did make some money from gambling.

Every time four ladies were present, they would *hoy toy,* which means "open the table." That term was used for *mahjong,* not for setting the table to eat. By the time I was seven years old, I often stayed up late at night to watch, until I was threatened with punishment if I didn't go to bed. This game totally fascinated me. It is a complicated game of half luck and half skill, and it is far more difficult to play than poker.

We received large crates of food (each about one foot by one foot by three feet) through the Swiss Red Cross every month or so. These crates contained chocolate, spam, sauerkraut, canned cheese, and a few other items. A bottle of vitamins was supposed to be included in one of the corners, but it was always missing. We suspected that the Japanese soldiers took them during inspection.

The Swiss Red Cross gave tuition money for Charlie and Maria to go to a Chinese school. At that time, Japanese was taught each day to all children in these schools. I believe my mother received some additional money from the Swiss Red Cross to support the family. I don't know if we would have survived without this help, which we remember with gratitude. This humanitarian organization also took care of Australian and British children whose parents were in the concentration camp like my father.

I remember receiving these crates because the large sauerkraut can, when opened by my mother, gave off a terrible smell. This, in addition to the fact that the can was puffed up, made her believe that the contents were spoiled. One time my uncle (the husband of my mother's sister) who was a chief engineer on a ship and was a world traveler, saw this and showed my mother how to cook the sauerkraut, because it was a vegetable with a lot of nutrients (especially Vitamin C) that all of us desperately needed. In those days we mainly ate plain *congee* (rice gruel) in the morning, with a skimpy meal at noon. There was no food for dinner.

The canned cheese (being an unfamiliar food item) also took some getting used to in our family. My uncle relished it, and he wanted to show us a special way to eat it—melted over a dish of cooked cauliflower. We thought he had ruined our meal.

About once a week during 1943/44, the Flying Tigers from Chunking would come and bomb Shanghai. We used to joke that every time our mother cooked sweet red-bean soup we would get bombed by the Americans. While she and her friends or relatives were playing *mahjong,* my brother Charlie and I would sneak out to watch the fireworks. As half-Americans we were thrilled to see our "half-brothers" strike at the Japanese. I had great admiration for those pilots and not surprisingly it made me want to become a pilot myself.

The noise of the explosions was our cue to climb the stairs that led to the roof. The sirens would usually go off late, after the bombs had fallen, and Charlie and I commented that the sirens were a send-off for the bombers. Our roof was flat, with a jumble of things stored there as well as laundry hung out to dry. Thus we were able to hide without being caught.

After we returned to the apartment from the rooftop, we would simulate an airplane by placing a plank crosswise on a sturdy bench. With Charlie sitting on one end of the plank and me on the other as bombardiers, we would invent English words and tell each other in Chinese what they meant. For example, *karabom* was "bombs away"—we did not know how to speak English during those years.

When the bombing was at night, we had to draw all the window shades. The whole city would be dark, except for the *ack-ack* guns and searchlights that lit up the sky. The Japanese had placed the guns in populated areas, and one of the guns was right across the street from us on the roof of a movie theatre.

Because I was always hungry, I would sneak out at night during blackout and scavenge for bits of food at a nearby market. I would hit a different stall each time and grab a handful of dumplings, a spring roll, or even a piece of barbecued pork from a pot, then run to a hiding place and quickly gulp down whatever I happened to snare. After a while, Charlie joined me on these forays, and one time Maria begged us to take her along. But she was almost caught, and also my mother started to get suspicious. Thus I decided to stop these risky excursions. My behavior was not unique. Many hungry children with clawing pain in their bellies were driven to search for food and steal, especially during the cover of total darkness every time bombs were falling on many parts of the city from the Flying Tigers. We were like desperate starving little rats.

Sometime in late 1944 or early 1945, when Charlie and I were on the rooftop during one of those bomb runs, we noticed a Flying Tiger P-51 go down in smoke. I believe these P-51s were escorts for the B-25 and B-29 bombers. We did not see the pilot bail out. A day or two later, we were confronted with a horrible scene that is still etched in my mind. An American pilot with a rope binding his hands was dragged behind a truck through Bubbling Well Road. I am not sure if he was dead or alive. A loudspeaker kept blaring from the truck how this American had come to kill Chinese civilians. From that day on, my brother and I stopped watching the bombing.

In late August 1945, we knew something was afoot when we saw Japanese troops leave their posts along Bubbling Well Road. Rumors were flying about an invasion. One evening, the phone rang in our building—we had one phone for four families—and the person answering the phone screamed and then whispered that the Japanese had surrendered. We could not believe it. We were afraid to even say it because the Japanese soldiers had killed entire families at the least sign of disrespect. One of our uncles (my mother's second brother) died from the effects of a savage beating he had received at the hands of the Japanese soldiers.

Although as children we understood that the United States had zapped Japan with a humongous "bright-bomb," we did not have a clue as to what that was. It was totally beyond our comprehension that two atom bombs were dropped with ferocious destructive power, one on Hiroshima on August 6 and one on Nagasaki three days later.

The day after the astounding news of the Japanese surrender, Charlie, Maria and I brought forth a large US flag that we had painted years earlier when our father was taken to the concentration camp. We glued the flag onto a long bamboo pole used for drying laundry and stuck it out the small attic window. When our mother saw it, she ordered us to instantly bring the flag inside, since Japanese troops were still patrolling the city. She then tore it into bits and burned them in our cook stove. She tried to soothe us by saying, "You can buy a new flag when your father returns home."

These optimistic words were unexpected, because by this time, we did not know if our father was dead or alive. Many years later, during family get-togethers, we would chuckle about the flag incident and quip, "Mom must have been the first American flag burner."

After the formal Japanese surrender on September 2, it took about a week for all their troops to leave Shanghai. Father came home a day or two later. All I remember about that day is my surprise that he was a white man and so very tall and skinny. I had seen him only twice early in his internment. Once, Mom was allowed a visit, and she took Charlie and me along, the other time was through a chain-link fence as we walked by the camp. After about thirty months since then I had forgotten what he looked like.

He never talked about the years of his internment—the memories were simply unspeakable. Charlie and Maria have told me that from that time on our father was never again the same man they had known as small children. Many years later, I took my family to see *Empire of the Sun,* a 1987 Steven Spielberg movie based on the 1984 J.G. Ballard novel, to give them a sense of what life was like in these Japanese internment camps.

The weeks between the Japanese departure and the Nationalist troops entering the city were a time of anarchy and lawlessness, with bands of thugs roaming Shanghai. Charlie and I picked up many live bullets and shells. When I found an unusually fat bullet, my brother alarmed me by saying, "This one will explode upon entering a body." I quickly handed it to him. Two large spent shells we passed on to a cousin who turned them into ashtrays.

Nationalists under Chiang Kai-Shek and Communists under Mao Zedong were scrambling to seize territory and armament left by the Japanese. The Americans intervened and sent 50,000 troops from the Asian theater into China. Many came to Shanghai to restore order. These troops waited for the occupying Chinese Nationalist forces of Chiang Kai-Shek to establish a government. Charlie and I got rid of our cache of ammunition once the Nationalist troops began to arrive.

We loved the US troops, but one incident gives me goose bumps even this day when I think about it. I was walking on

Bubbling Well Road with a group of kids from the apartments in our lane, when a sailor ambling by said a few badly pronounced words in Mandarin that made us giggle. Presumably because I looked different from the others in my group, he took me by the hand and started walking with me down the road. I was scared but happy to be "the chosen one." He fed me and gave me chocolate.

Then he led me to the area where the singsong girls were—the prostitution and opium district (I did not learn this until years later). He took me to the second floor of a building and motioned for me to stay put while he walked over to a Chinese man. They were making conversation, with the sailor occasionally pointing at me. The Chinese man kept looking at me and periodically shook his head.

The sailor argued and finally threw up his hands. He walked over to me, smacked me on the head, and motioned for me to scoot. I left thinking that I had done something to offend him or that there was something wrong with me, and these feelings of low self-worth stayed with me for some time. Years later I heard that many boys and girls were sold into slavery there.

Father, after release from the concentration camp, could have had free passage to the US for himself and his family aboard the *President Wilson* of the American President Lines. Although he had lost his business because of the war, he chose to stay in China, where he had already lived for seventeen years. He thought it unlikely that he could find a good job in the US. But because he was a *guay tzu*, he was able to get a well-paid position with American President Lines in Shanghai. Although he did not show it through hugs or words, I am convinced that he loved my mother and wanted to raise their children in China.

We now could afford two servants. These *goong yan* lived with us and did everything from cleaning to washing clothes and caring for the babies and toddlers in the growing family. They also helped my mother and grandmother with the daily cooking and grocery shopping. In the West, Chinese servants are commonly called *ahmahs,* but we never used that term.

3
Gambit: Early School Years

I had been sent to a Chinese school when I was seven. But at the start of second grade I had a bad fall down the stairs in our apartment building, giving me a prodigious nosebleed. My mother and grandmother took this as an omen—they feared something worse would happen to me at school, and thus I was kept home the entire school year.

In 1946, I first went to a Jewish school where we had to pray in Hebrew. I mimicked the words but didn't have a clue as to what I was saying. Classes in Yiddish also were a mystery. But when the Jesuit Brothers opened two Catholic schools, Charlie and I, as well as my younger brother George, were enrolled at St. Joan of Arc.

Maria told our father that she wanted to learn English. She found Santa Sophia, a Russian Greek Orthodox girl school. During registration, the nuns named her Maria, not liking Yao-tim as being pagan. But when Maria realized she did not like this school, she searched again and found Loretto School run by American nuns. Maria went there until she left China in 1951.

Saint Joan of Arc had mostly foreigners and half-Chinese like me who were "not fit" to go to the regular Chinese school. My parents felt we would receive a far better education and discipline with the Jesuits, but for me, it was the start of a bent for gambling.

At St. Joan of Arc I met my gambling partners. Two of them were Jackie Howard and Harry Woodhouse, both half

Chinese. Although we gambled mostly with cards (blackjack) and dice, Jackie was the con-boy who often won. The others could pay Jackie for their losses, but I did not have the money. Two friends did not gamble: Albert Gersberg and Alex Poljak. I thought they were Russian Jews (or White Russians) whose families escaped to China because of the Red Russians or Bolsheviks—later known as Communists.

The photo shows Brother Jimboom with my class at St. Joan of Arc. In the back, Jackie Howard is third from the left; I'm third from the right.

Jackie was much brawnier than any of us and would frequently threaten me. One day he even got two of his friends, known as the mean Barradas brothers, to come after me. I was beaten up. When I got home I told my mother I had fallen while playing soccer during recess. But Jackie had put the fear of God in me.

From that time on, my life was anything but blissful. Jackie continued to pressure me daily to pay him. I tried several different ways to earn money. The first one was by "scalping" theatre tickets. The nearly disastrous outcome that ended my venture is recounted at the start of this book.

Gambit: Early School Years

I was forbidden to ask my friend Yu-Ming who lived upstairs in our building for help, so I desperately had to look elsewhere for another enterprise. The photo below of our lane (#1168 Bubbling Well Road) was taken about forty years later when I made a visit. Small shops still fronted the street and a large gate closed it off to traffic. I was surprised that nothing much had changed; even a loose brick by the door was still there. But by 1997, these tenements had been replaced by modern high-rise buildings.

After a few days, when walking home from school on Avenue Joffre in what used to be the French Concession, I noticed a fairly large new store selling chocolate, candy, chewing gum, and other sundries at about half the price being charged at a small store just outside my lane. I smelled an opportunity.

I asked the lane storekeeper if he would buy sundries at

a price I knew would make a profit for me. He was interested, and he wrote down the quantities he wanted of each. However, I needed to bring the goods first, before he would pay me.

Without the necessary funds and unable to tell my father about all these shenanigans because I saw him as a fierce *bak guay*, I went back to Yu-Min, my venture capitalist. We sold more shirts, and I bought a large quantity of goods as specified by the lane storekeeper. Then with what he paid me, we went to the clothing store to buy back shirts. The old man was willing to sell—for about fifty percent more than the price he had paid us. I had only enough money to buy back roughly half the shirts.

For weeks, I continued to check with the storekeeper to see if he needed more goods, since I had to buy more shirts and was desperate to pay Jackie. The storekeeper always shooed me away. But one day he said, *"Pao gao* ('running dog'), I want more goods."

"I need to borrow money from you to buy the merchandise," I proposed, tentatively.

To my surprise he loaned it to me this time. When I returned with the goods, he happily paid my commission. Badly fearing a black eye or worse, I now paid some money to Jackie.

I thought I had an established business at age ten. But the next time I stopped by to ask the storekeeper if he needed more goods, he snapped, *"Tzoe* (buzz off)."

Rather puzzled, I asked, "Why?"

He explained, "I'm no fool. Last time, when I loaned you the money, I followed you to your supplier. So now I can buy my own goods—I no longer need a running dog."

That was the sudden end of my second venture.

Meanwhile, noticing that I had been able to get hold of money to pay my gambling debts, Jackie tempted me into a hot upcoming blackjack game with Harry Woodhouse and an American kid who was the son of a Navy commander. This Jeffrey Murdock was a student at St. Joan of Arc and was loaded (compared to us). Jackie said I could easily win what I still owed him, as Jeff was a sucker. In a way, I felt a kinship with Jackie and Harry—all three of us were biracial and thus neither accepted by the Chinese nor the Americans—so I was easily persuaded and looked forward to taking this American to the cleaners.

We got into a game outside the Avenue Joffre Theatre. On the manicured lawn, Jackie laid out a cloth and took out his deck of cards. Jeff lost a bundle and, as Jackie had predicted, the three of us won. I did not win enough to pay Jackie off, but it helped to reduce the debt. Over the next few weeks, Jeff had his ups and downs, but mostly downs. Harry was up some, but I kept losing, and my debt with Jackie increased. I felt stupid for owing Jackie ever more money while still having to buy back more shirts for Yu-Min's father. Also, I had no other prospects of income.

Chinese New Year came around and we all received *hung bao*, the traditional red wrappers with money. My uncle, the chief engineer, was always very generous with me since I was his favorite nephew. Whenever he heard my mother criticizing me, he predicted that I would make something of myself. This year he gave me a watch and enough money to pay most of what I owed to Jackie.

A few days later I sold the watch to buy back more shirts. I felt really bad about selling my uncle's watch, because he was the one man in my life then who always stood up for me.

Desperately looking for another opportunity to earn money, I noticed a long queue every other day at a Russian bakery shop outside our lane. From 1946 to 1949, this shop did a phenomenal business. Many of our friends and acquaintances would line up to buy bread, and those who could afford servants, including Alex Poljak's mother, would send them to stand in line. Our family, however, only rarely ate bread; we customarily had *congee* for breakfast—porridge made by boiling the crusty leftover rice from the previous day.

One afternoon, I asked some of the people I knew in the queue if they would like their bread delivered for a small fee. We negotiated the price. I started my delivery service using my bike, and it grew until I had about thirty customers. I did not even need venture capital for this business since I would take my customers' order and money, buy the bread, and get the commission when I delivered their purchases, always on time.

After a few weeks, I wanted to buy back more shirts to return to Yu-Min but couldn't—the old man had sold the rest. So Yu-Min and I bought five new shirts from a department store near the Bund and had a servant at a friend's house wash and press them, thinking his father would not know the difference. However, a few days later, Yu-Min came to me with an "empty-stomach" face. He confirmed my worst fears: "My father returned and discovered he had neither the right number nor the right kind of shirts. I had no choice but to confess everything."

The next day when we were playing kick-the-can in the lane, Yu-Min's father came up to me and sternly commanded, "Come with me." He talked to me in colloquial Putonghua, as the family was originally from Suchow (Xuzhou).

As we entered his apartment, he scolded me: "You are

corrupting my son. I order you to stay away from him."

I held my breath, not knowing what he would do to me about the theft.

He looked at the scar on my forehead for a moment, and his stern face relaxed. "I will not do anything further about the matter of the shirts, because my older son shot you between the eyes with a BB gun earlier this year, and now we are even." Then he handed me the five shirts Yu-Min and I had bought, as they were not his size.

Greatly relieved, I scampered out of the apartment. I went directly to the old man and sold him the five shirts. Yu-Min and I remained good friends (but not business partners) until I left Shanghai.

My delivery service worked well, and I did not have competition. It helped me pay Jackie and allowed me to buy treats, a favorite being *tucks*: Chinese dried plums, mangoes and the like. When a rash of small thefts occurred at my school, I was accused of being the culprit because I suddenly had lots of *tucks*, firecrackers, and kites. However, I was able to prove to Brother Gilbert, the headmaster, that I had earned the money with my delivery service. In fact, I had seen one of the Barradas brothers take money from a student's jacket, but I was too scared of their revenge to report it to anyone.

I remember the period from 1946 to 1948 as a time when our family had plenty to eat. Many Americans were in the city, as well as an increasing number of Nationalist soldiers with rifles that looked exactly like those the Japanese had carried during their occupation. In those days, Shanghai was known as the Paris of the East. It had everything for the adventurer, from many *guay tzu* millionaires to thugs, revolutionaries and mobsters like Du Yuesheng, the Al Capone of China. Moreover, the beautiful starlet and politically ambitious Jiang Qing was living in Shanghai. She later became Madame Mao Zedong.

The photo below was taken during this relatively prosperous time. The cocky smile sets me apart from my serious father and siblings Charlie, Maria, and George.

In 1948, the economy in Shanghai as well as in all of China turned turbulent as the Communist takeover—or liberation, depending on which side you were on—became more imminent. By that time Mao's Eighth Route Army had already taken much of the north and was marching towards Shanghai. Banners were hung everywhere proclaiming Communists as murderers of children and yes, as running dogs for the Soviets. American soldiers and sailors were no longer a common sight.

From late 1948 to early 1949, money literally was not worth the paper it was printed on. My father would come home on payday with a sack full of new bills. A stack of bills was needed just to buy some rice. It was customary to look at the serial numbers of the first and last bill to tell how much was in the stack (with a flip through the stack as a check)—counting each bill would have taken too long.

Possessing precious metals, changing money, and using foreign currency were now strictly prohibited, and money-changers were regularly executed. A moneychanger lived in our lane. He used to joke with the children and seemed like a very nice man. I remember his arrest one afternoon by a few plainclothes police. We never saw him again.

4
Life under the Communists

Sometime in April 1949, we started to hear artillery outside the city. People by the thousands were flocking to the city's center from the outskirts. Two families who knew my mother came to stay with us. This made more than thirty people crammed into three rooms. Also, our lane had to house and feed several Nationalist soldiers. These soldiers were retreating from the Communists and were supposed to defend the city. Curfew was very strict, and anyone found in the streets after curfew was arrested or shot.

One morning one of the soldiers told us a drunken American sailor was almost killed because he kept on walking when ordered in Chinese to halt. When the soldier realized he was dealing with an American and not a Communist infiltrator, he used his *kung fu* on the sailor to wrestle him to the ground and arrest him. We were all very impressed when he demonstrated his martial arts to us. However, on the day when his comrades were engaged in a gun battle in the streets near us, he chose to be a live coward rather than a dead hero—we saw him slip into civilian clothes and stealthily disappear into the streets.

Then the artillery went silent. A few days later, the street fighting started. One morning we were awakened to the sound of hand grenades and machine gunfire right across the street from us. For a time, there was more shouting than noise of battle—through bullhorns, the Communists "encouraged" the Nationalists to give up rather than fight

Life under the Communists

against their brothers. After a few more hours of only sporadic gunfire, the streets became eerily silent. In our building crammed full of people, only whispers could be heard throughout the entire day.

The next morning dawned crisp and cloudless. Charlie and I were curious about the silence. We wanted to go out of the lane early to see what was happening. Two big steel gates closed off our lane from Bubbling Well Road. But it was possible to go in or out through a small iron door alongside the gates, and a watchman for the entire lane had a little shack close to the iron door.

As we unlatched the little door, the watchman stopped us. With his shaved head, he looked ferocious, so we decided to retreat. A few hours later, people were starting to go out into the streets. We took a chance and slipped out behind a group, unseen.

Outside the lane, we observed column after column of soldiers walking through the streets. They neither seemed battle-weary nor marched in step. At first my brother and I looked at each other and decided it must be that the Nationalists were retreating. Then someone pointed to the red star on the cap of one of the soldiers and said, *"goong tzahn dong."* We ran back into the apartment and proudly reported that the Communists had now taken over the city.

In October 1949, Mao Zedong proclaimed the People's Republic of China at Tien An Men Square in Beijing with his now famous wave to the people from the top of the main gate. What was unbelievable to me and my older siblings were the daily executions that now occurred.

Trials were conducted all over Shanghai. They were open to the public, and anyone could accuse anyone else at these trials. Every morning, large open trucks crammed full of prisoners rumbled down Bubbling Well Road on the way to the execution ground at the old racecourse. The prisoners had their hands tied behind their backs, and a long white board sticking up from their backs declared in Chinese characters the name and the offense for which these unfortunate people were to be executed.

The trials were quick and the judgment swift—most times, execution followed the day after the trial. Occasionally, someone would beg for mercy, but the tribunal (usually three officers) would wave to the waiting soldiers as if telling them to remove some garbage. I will never forget the look of horror on the faces of some of the prisoners. Many of them had been well-to-do until the Communist takeover. It was rumored the spent bullet used in each execution was sent to the family—they were asked to pay the government for the price of the bullet. China scholars have estimated that the number of executions in the early years of Communist rule was in the millions.

Sometime in 1950, our family was again given a chance to go to America on the *President Wilson*. It was a difficult decision for my father who knew that in the US he would not enjoy the same prestige he had in China—likely, only menial jobs would be open to him. But he decided we should all go. I believe the decision was based on his concern for his children's health—there were a multitude of diseases in Shanghai at the time.

However, the day before our scheduled departure, two of my younger siblings came down with the mumps. Taking the illness as an omen, my mother convinced my father we should not leave Shanghai. My maternal grandmother (whose name was Liana Yee-Dai but I knew her as *Poh-poh*) was delighted because she would have been left behind. The two *goong yan* still with us were overjoyed, too.

A few weeks later, my youngest brother was born, and a few months after that, grandmother died in her sleep. This came as a shock since she had not appeared to be ill. The

photo was taken a few weeks earlier. I mourned her loss deeply but silently—I felt she had been the only one in my family who had unfailingly stood up for me.

During the early months of 1951, I sensed something was very wrong. My father would become moody and irritated even with music he normally enjoyed. One afternoon I came in from playing in the lane after school and sat on one of our wood stools in the house. My father walked into the room and asked who had turned on the radio—a waltz was playing. Charlie accused me. Despite my denial, I received a severe spanking. The more I protested, the harder my father whacked my behind.

Other signs showed he was disturbed. By May, he began to jump out of bed in the middle of the night. Rushing to the window overlooking the lane, he would hold onto the grille like a prisoner. My mother later told us he was breaking out in cold sweat. Sometimes we would hear him scream in his sleep, mixing Cantonese and Mandarin, "*Tah men lay lie ng'or* (They are coming for me)!" He was referring to the Communists, of course, but his mind was flashing back to the years of horror while interned by the Japanese during the Second World War.

The family photo above was taken around that time. Charlie is the tallest because he is standing on a small stool between Maria and me. In the front from left to right are Robert, Philip, Dolly, Albert, Milly and George.

By mid-year, demonstrations by different groups carrying banners broadcasting "Down with U.S.A." and calling America a paper tiger became frequent occurrences. Also, the Nationalist leader Chiang Kai-shek, who retreated to Formosa, was America's "running dog." Since Formosa (now called Taiwan) was being protected by the Seventh Fleet and the Communists did not have a navy or air force, they did not want to confront the US except with rhetoric. At that time, Russia was China's staunch ally. The Chinese Communists called the Russian Communists "Big Brother." However, the USSR had just come through a devastating World War and was in no mood to challenge the mighty military power of the US in the Far East.

Things got progressively worse as my father slid into deep depression. None of us understood what was happening. Many missionaries and Catholic priests had left Shanghai by this time, and some were arrested. American President Lines were closing their offices in Shanghai, and my father lost his job. I now think that he must have lived in constant fear that the Communists might arrest him.

Because of these deteriorating conditions by August 1951, and at my mother's repeated urging, my father decided to leave for the US, taking Charlie with him. This was very hard for my parents since my mother would be left with eight children to care for. My father took the last of the family's savings to pay for the passage. Nonetheless, they were confident my father would get a job, earn enough money and soon send for the rest of us. We all made it to the US in the end, but the process was much longer and more difficult—and in my case much more adventurous—than we could have imagined. The family would not be reunited until ten years later.

Ironically, upon his return to the US, my father was accused of being a Communist. He lost one job after another, not knowing the McCarthy era witch hunters had him blacklisted. Behind his back the FBI and CIA were investigating him. Only in 2002, under the Freedom of Information Act, did my sister Dolly receive a 30-page FBI document. What I read made me very, very angry about the years of unjust persecution my father suffered for nothing more than being outspoken and unable to cope with the culture shock when transplanted back to the US. The loss of respect he felt due to his inability to hold a good job hurt him deeply. It also influenced my future—getting a top job and making lots of money to support my family became my driving priority which ultimately spiraled into a pattern of workaholism.

After my father left for the United States, I grew more and more unmanageable. I would skip school to go roller-skating with my school chum Gersberg. Periodically, I bought large quantities of writing tablets from St. Joan of Arc to sell to the corner stand for a profit. Then I spent the money on *tucks*, roller-skating at the rink and payments to Jackie whom I tried to avoid as much as possible.

Brother Gilbert as headmaster would dish out punishment every Monday to those who had "unsatisfactory conduct" on their report cards issued each Friday. He used a rigid whip to regularly tan my behind—five sharp whacks were the standard. One Monday I decided to outsmart him. I placed paper and a thin towel between my underwear and pants. After one whack that sounded like a dull thump, Brother Gilbert ordered me to remove my pants and underwear, and he finished the job on my bare bottom. I was unable to sit down for a day or two—a terrible embarrassment—and my classmates were merciless in making fun of me.

My writing tablet sales soon came to a halt. One day,

when I showed up at the school store window to buy another stockpile, Brother Gilbert ordered me to see him in his office. There, he told me sternly he was sure all the writing tablets I was buying were not for personal use, since I was falling behind academically and he saw no evidence I was working hard at my studies. In fact, I was absent so much he wanted me to take a note to my parents—he did not yet know my father had left Shanghai. The note, which I had to translate for my mother, requested that my parents meet with Brother Gilbert.

At the meeting the next day, Brother Gilbert informed my mother through a translator that I was to be expelled from the school since I played hooky, fought constantly, and set a terrible example for the other students. My mother, sobbing, explained that even though she spanked me, I was very disrespectful and unruly at home as well. I learned later that Albert Gersberg was also expelled, but his parents were well-to-do and claimed I was the bad influence. They apologized profusely for their son who was a "very good boy." As a result, he was quickly readmitted.

The other Jesuit school, St. Francis Xavier, was located on the far side of Shanghai where my uncle the engineer lived. Somehow, he got me into that school. However, my tarnished reputation followed me. Anytime there was an incident, like someone writing on a wall, I was blamed. I spent more hours staring at the blank walls in detention because of misconduct than learning in the classroom. Nevertheless, I maintained top scores in math and geography which saved me from utter disaster.

After a few months, I started to play hooky again. I began to take Alex Poljak into the countryside around Shanghai a few times to hunt for pheasants. Alex had two slug guns (similar to but more powerful than BB guns). We had no chance of bagging a pheasant but brought down a handful of smaller birds by sniping. Alex took these home to be cooked.

One day, Alex got bored and took potshots at passing pedicabs. He nicked the leg of a pedicab driver, and the two passengers promptly took us to the police station. Alex's father, a wealthy Russian, bailed us out and gave the pedicab driver a big stash of money. The pedicab driver was in severe pain until he received the money; then he miraculously recovered and quickly rode off. Alex's father was rumored to belong to the Russian Communist party. No wonder we got off easy. But when my mother found out about the incident the next day, I received a whipping.

At about this time, our mother decided to send Maria to join our father in the US, hoping she would be able to help him out of his depression. My mother needed to take Maria to Hong Kong and then find a ship for her for San Francisco. Since Maria was born in Hong Kong, she could return there. They had to borrow money for the train fare to Hong Kong, where they tried for about a month to raise funds for the ship fare. Maria was able to get a US passport without a problem, and she borrowed money from an American doctor for our mother's train fare to return to Shanghai.

As I found out much later, Father DesLauriers, a Catholic priest, then lent her the money for her ship passage. A group of Jesuit priests returning to the US chaperoned Maria on the ship, a Swedish freighter. Within a year or so, she met and married a US sailor. I believe it is their common faith that has helped their marriage prosper to this day.

Primarily our two *goong yan* took care of me and my younger siblings while our mother was away. Her sister, who was busy with her own family and lived some distance away, would only occasionally stop by to check on us.

By mid-1952, I was under a lot of stress from trying to complete the equivalent of seventh grade at St. Francis Xavier. I felt trapped and wanted to be on my own. The Communists had arrested two of my cousins (older brothers of the one who had taught me to swim)—they were suspected of being Nationalist sympathizers. They were sent to work on a dam at some far off place, and I never saw them again. I feared that I might be next since my rebellious conduct was not up to Communist standards.

I wanted desperately to go to America. I dreamed I would be free there and knew that everyone could become rich. In fact, San Francisco was called *jiu jin shan* (Old Gold Mountain) in Mandarin, and New York was called *sun gum shan* (New Gold Mountain). But my father and brother in California could barely scrape up enough money for us to live on, much less pay for my passage. It never occurred to me to ask, if everyone could become rich in the United States, why didn't my father and brother rake in some of those riches?

Thus, at fourteen—yearning with every fiber of my body for the American dream—I decided to leave Shanghai and find my own way to "Old Gold Mountain," though I didn't even have enough money to pay for the train to Hong Kong. I would eventually discover that it was not America that would satisfy my yearnings. My life journey turned out to be quite different from what I expected—I could never have imagined in my wildest dreams the peaks I would reach or the pit of despair I would slide into before my soul found true freedom and contentment.

5
Escaping Shanghai

Looking back on those years in Shanghai, I don't know how we survived. At one point, my parents, nine children, my cousin Ho Siu Hwa, grandmother and her close friend, and two *goong yan* all lived together in less than 1,000 square feet. We had one toilet and a huge wooden tub for occasional baths—perhaps once a week in summer and once a month in winter. We did use a small towel to wash our face, neck, and underarms daily.

The *goong yan* and three children slept on folding cots. The youngest slept with the parents, the other children two to a bed in the parents' room. I had slept with my grandmother until I was nine; then I slept on a mat in the storage attic, which was reached by a ladder. Its ceiling was so low that I could not sit up.

We had no cooling, and we had heating only when it was very cold. Then, a potbelly stove was fired up with coal, and heat was distributed with the pipes running along the ceiling. In my attic cubby I sweated in the buff in the summer, and in the winter I used a very thick quilt to keep warm. A few times, we had lice, and all our clothes would have to be boiled.

We hunted for the abundant red bed bugs at least once a week. Once I woke out of a deep sleep with a terrible buzz-sawing sound in my ear. Frantically I tried to shake the intruder out, but to no avail. In the dark, I found my way to the outdoor kitchen and got hold of a sharp straw which I poked into my ear. This encouraged the bed bug to crawl out of my ear. It is a wonder I did not break my ear drum.

The kitchen was shared by the two families who lived on the ground floor. We raised half a dozen chickens in the kitchen, and we kids excitedly volunteered to take turns searching for the eggs. There were no cats, and I don't remember seeing any rats. We brought home a stray dog once and had it for a couple of months, but because it barked, someone poured hot water on it. One of my cousins who frequently visited us—and who later died of TB at twenty-six, when I was twelve—begged us to let him take care of the dog. We never saw the dog again.

We caught just about every imaginable childhood disease. In the winter, we suffered from vitamin deficiency with boils between our fingers, especially during the war. I saw a doctor only once—for a physical exam—during my eleven years in Shanghai, and I never saw a dentist. Both my mother and grandmother gave us herbs for fever and colds, *Tiger Balm* for stomachaches, and a black gooey patch that smelled like camphor, or a mustard plaster, for aches and pains. Except for Charlie, all of us children were born at home. When family members needed months of hospitalization (George, Maria and especially Charlie), this added a great financial burden.

During the war years, it never occurred to us that we were poor, even though we sometimes ate only one meal a day plus *congee* for breakfast. In 1949 when the Communists were pushing their way into Shanghai, two families from the outskirts of Shanghai—friends of my mother—came to stay with us because we lived in the International Concession and the war was raging near their homes. Their children kept making sarcastic comments about how poor we were, and they made fun of our taking our rare baths in the wooden tub. This was the first time I was ashamed of our living conditions.

By 1952, the political climate increasingly made me feel anxious and restless—I simply *had* to find a way to escape Shanghai. My mother, fearing I would turn into a hooligan, told me to work with one of my many cousins in the evening because he was a skilled electrical technician. The Communist government had assigned him the job of fixing hundreds (maybe even thousands) of motor-generator sets in several warehouses. My cousin was a very kind man in his mid-twenties. Evening after evening, I would watch and help him as a gofer. I don't know if I helped very much.

One evening, he came to our apartment with a rice sack and sat on one of the benches, inviting me to sit next to him. He took out four very large U-shaped magnets, iron strip plates, several small gears, copper wires, a small light bulb, and a hand drill. He said in Cantonese, *"Ng'or gau neh dee-deen hi-uh bean doe lay-the* (I will teach you where electricity comes from)." He spent nearly seven hours working with me and explaining each step. I was fascinated. He showed me how the copper coil cut the magnetic field, thereby causing a current to flow through the coil to the light bulb. He drew the motion of the electrons and an electrical circuit. I thought: what a genius! He is partly responsible for my later wanting to become an engineer.

When he was finished building this mini-generator, it was a piece of art. Then he gave it to me! I could have hugged him, but in China it is not customary to hug even close family members—one shows affection very reservedly. I only recall my mother hugging me once, and my father was on his deathbed before I was able to tenderly hold his hand. And I have rarely hugged my siblings, even to this day. So with several timid bows I thanked my cousin. He seemed content I showed such admiration for his work.

To raise money for my journey to America, I started to sell whatever possessions I had. One item was my cousin's generator. I went to a store that sold used hardware and numerous electrical products. When I showed the storekeeper the generator and how it worked, he was intrigued. "Before I buy it, I need to talk this over with my partner first," he said as he reached for it.

I waited nearly two hours, with people streaming in and out of the store. Periodically I would ask, "What is happening with my generator?"

The reply was always, "Just be patient."

Finally, a man arrived who brought my generator with him. I was surprised because I had not seen anyone leave with it. The man had a Mao jacket on and a bulge in the jacket that was undoubtedly a gun. His whole demeanor declared him to be a plainclothes policeman. This was unsettling—these Communist police could whisk away anyone at any time without a charge.

After the storekeeper finished talking to the policeman, he beckoned me to the counter to give me a measly amount of money for the generator—much less than I had expected. I later found out he had called the police who then took the generator to my home and asked my mother if she recognized the device. Luckily, my mother had seen my cousin give it to me. So she said, "It belongs to one of my sons." I shudder what would have happened to me if she had not been able to testify to this fact. I might have been sent away for years of hard labor or worse—in those days, many petty thieves were arrested and never returned. Although I had done nothing wrong, I felt the world was closing in on me.

Two of my older friends (seventeen and eighteen) lived in our lane, and the older boy had taught me how to play the harmonica well. Now, in June 1952, at the peak of the Korean War, they suddenly decided to join the People's Liberation Army, and they were soon being trained to go to Korea to fight the *may kuo-tz lao foo* (American "paper tiger"). Shortly before they left, a large group of people came into our lane with gongs and drums to acclaim them as heroes of the revolution.

During this time, hostile feelings against Americans were rising—they were once again portrayed as the bad guys. Large posters in many stores accused the US of using biological weapons in Korea. Pictures of priests in their rooms with forbidden radios and transmitters proclaimed they were spies.

My brother Charlie, before he left for the US, used to regularly shellac an obnoxious Chinese boy in the neighborhood. Now the boy boldly took to cursing and calling us "bastard Americans." This was adding to my feelings of impending doom—and day after day I was plotting on how I could engineer my escape.

Although by this time I had sold everything I owned, it was not nearly enough to pay for the train ticket to Hong Kong. Over several days, I mulled over a new plan, one involving church. My siblings and I used to attend the Church of Christ the King, but after I was expelled from St. Joan of Arc, I had stopped going to church. The Communists, although making constant attempts to discredit all religions, had not yet imprisoned or expelled pastors and priests nor closed the churches—deadly persecution would come two years later.

At the Church of Christ the King one Sunday early in July 1952, I walked from the sanctuary to an adjacent building after mass. I asked to see Father Peter whom I thought to be the priest in charge. Too tense to sit, I paced around the small waiting room. Then a very tall and skinny man with wavy brown hair entered—Father Peter.

I blurted out, "I want to borrow money from you so I can take a train to Hong Kong. I want to work there and save enough to buy my passage to America."

At first Father Peter looked surprised, but then he asked me, "Were you in church this morning, and did you pray?"

Of course I said yes most emphatically—I had been in church, true, but I had been thinking all morning of what to say to him, instead of praying. He saw right through my pretense. Gently holding my hand, he asked me to pray with him, saying the Hail Mary and the Lord's Prayer.

Father Peter asked me to wait while he stepped into another room. When he reappeared, he held money in one hand and a note in the other. Handing me the money—which was more than the amount needed for the ticket to Hong Kong—he said, "You don't need to repay me, but be a good steward in how you use money and your opportunities. I will pray for you to be successful." At least this is what I understood he had said because my English was very poor. In my head I was repeating over and over, *I got the money, I got the money.* I was also thinking about the next step, getting my exit visa from the Communist government.

Then Father Peter handed me the note. "This is for Father DesLauriers, but everybody calls him Father Des. It is very likely he will have some work for you." The address and phone number were on the outside of the note.

Father Peter never asked who I was or what I believed. I had never seen him before and never saw him again. Years later, I inquired about Father Peter in Hong Kong, and I was told by more than one source that he never made it out of Mainland China. But since then, whenever I have a flashback to my meeting with Father Peter, my eyes invariably tear up, thinking on how this kind and generous priest totally changed my life. I see him as a true example of Christian love and representative of Jesus Christ. I have started to feel ashamed at the times in my adult life when I did not measure up. However, remembering Father Peter and his prayers now gives me hope and strength to overcome my failings.

The next day, one of my cousins took me to the police station to apply for an exit visa. Even though I was not quite fifteen, my name had to be published in the Shanghai newspaper for three days before I could be issued a visa. This process took two weeks, including a one-week waiting period. If anyone came forward and claimed I owed money, had said something counter-revolutionary, had committed a crime, or was suspected of being a thief or spy, I would be denied a visa and prosecuted.

I was terrified. I was certain someone would appear to say I fought all the time and was expelled from school, or Jackie Howard would report I owed him money. Fortunately, no one informed on me. Of course, looking back I believe the Communists were glad to rid China of another *guay tzu* with or without a criminal record.

At the end of July I had two essential documents in hand: the exit visa and my birth certificate proving I was born in Kowloon, a city that was part of the British Colony of Hong Kong. Now I was able to purchase a one-way ticket to Lo

Wu, the station at the border of Communist China. Based on my birth certificate, I could enter and stay in Hong Kong for an indefinite period.

My mother and her sister accompanied me to the train station. A young woman from our lane and her child were also going to be on the train, since she was on her way to join her husband in Kowloon. My mother told me to call her *ah-yee* ("auntie").

As I was waiting in line to board the train, my aunt began to cry. She asked my mother, "Are you sad to see your son leave all by himself at such a young age?"

My mother simply responded, "He has become utterly unmanageable."

I did not outwardly react, even though her seemingly indifferent demeanor cut my heart—was she thinking, *I wish he had never been born?*

My mother then turned to me and said, "Look up your cousin Ho Siu Hwa, if you can't find a place to stay in Hong Kong—she might put you up. She moved to Hong Kong about four years ago and is now married." This talk was entirely in Cantonese, as neither my aunt nor my mother spoke any other language or dialect.

It was still about an hour before departure, but I was anxious to get on the train. Just as I was boarding, a Communist soldier took me by the arm and ordered me to accompany him. I was really scared—had it somehow been discovered that I was a bad boy?

As we walked for a few minutes to a shack with a group of plainclothes police, I was sure my next destination would be working on the dam with my cousins. But I was questioned because I was five foot ten (one of the tallest persons there) and also looked different with biracial facial features.

The soldier checked that all my papers were in order and then let me go.

As I boarded the train, my mother handed me four canisters that were joined together with flat rods and connected to a handle at the top. The Chinese use these metal canisters as lunch boxes for carrying rice and other dishes, with a quilted cover to keep the food warm. My mother warned

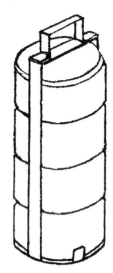

me, "There might not be food on the train, so don't eat it all at once like a *fahn toong* (which means 'rice bucket')."

With a smile I thanked her. Then she and my aunt left. When the train pulled out of the station, I felt a surge of immense anticipation and relief—I was ready for anything. I had some anxiety for sure, but no regrets or grief.

I shared a small compartment with the "auntie" and her child, as well as an elderly couple from Suchow. There were four wooden bench-bunks, about five feet long. I had the upper bunk and "auntie" with her baby the lower bunk on one side, with the couple in the bunks on the other side. The ride was hot all the way. Soldiers continuously patrolled the carriage corridors. When we were allowed to open the window, it was a relief, but each time we crossed a bridge we had to close it. Flies and mosquitoes added to the discomfort.

When I pulled the cover off the canisters, I found a note from my mother. She wanted to be sure I had cousin's address. She added that although I had been a troublesome son she wished me a good journey and urged me to make something out of my life. I was glad she had taken the time to have someone write the note for her—although she read Chinese she could not write. I began to think that perhaps I could have been less rebellious to make her life easier.

But I soon turned from my musings to investigate the content of the canisters. One was filled with rice, one with vegetable, and one with barbecued pork—my favorite which I ate first. The last one contained an assortment of *tucks*. The food lasted the entire two-day journey.

6
Hong Kong Interlude: A Way to America

What a relief it was when we finally arrived at Lo Wu Station, the end of the line for the train from Shanghai. After going through a border checkpoint and crossing a narrow bridge on foot, we entered the New Territories of the British Crown Colony of Hong Kong. "Auntie's" happy husband met us. He had bought tickets for all of us for the train ride to Kowloon. When we arrived there, he shook my hand in farewell and thanked me for taking care of his wife and child on the journey from Shanghai. Although I didn't expect him to invite me to dinner, I had hoped he would at least give me directions to my cousin's place or perhaps take me there.

For the first time in my life I felt very alone. I only had two small bags with some clothing; I only had the one pair of shoes I was wearing. Momentarily I had to lean against a tree and put my hands to my face. I recited by rote the two prayers I had been taught in school in Shanghai: Our Father and Hail Mary.

I did not have any Hong Kong dollars and had no idea how to exchange currency. I walked over to a cab and gave the driver my cousin's address, hoping when I arrived she would be there to pay the cab.

When the cab stopped, I found that the building had a watchman at a barred gate.

"I'm here to see my cousin Ho Siu Hwa and her husband on the eighth floor," I said, glancing at my mother's note. But the watchman refused to let me in. "Could you please call her on the phone or go up and tell her of my arrival," I pleaded.

He shook his head. "I cannot leave my post, and I don't have a phone."

Fortunately, another tenant overheard the conversation and was willing to go and inform my cousin. Within a few minutes, Ho Siu Hwa appeared. I was relieved to see her. She paid the cab and took me to what I thought was a very spacious apartment.

After providing me with a meal, she told me, "You can spend the night, but this is all I can do for you. Our place is small; I'm working as a nurse's aide; my husband James is without a job, and as you can see, I'm expecting a child."

Before I could argue about her decision, Ho Siu Hwa asked, "Do you know that you have another cousin who might put you up?" Without a pause, she continued, "Hung Tzer is not really related to our family. She is the fourth wife of a very wealthy man. When your father and Charlie were in Hong Kong on their way to the US last year, she took them in. And she did the same when your mother was in Hong Kong with Maria. Apparently, Hung Tzer is grateful to your family because her father had received large loans from your maternal grandfather before the war. Surely she would be happy to help you out as well."

Since Ho Siu Hwa had to work the next day, James took me to Hung Tzer's apartment building. The building was at Number 3 Nathan Road, and it was five stories high and entirely owned by Hung Tzer's husband. We rang a bell, and a guard came to the iron gate and opened a small barred window. After inspecting us, he left.

We waited awhile. Finally the guard returned with two

elderly *goong yan* in tow. They smiled when they saw me. "Let them in," they commanded the guard.

One of the *goong yan* turned to me and explained, "I used to work for your maternal grandfather before the war."

We were taken to an ornate room and served tea. Then James left.

When I was introduced to some of the younger servants, they giggled because my given name "I Hwa" (meaning "love China")—although patriotic—was a girl's name. My mother had phonetically translated into Chinese the English name my father had entered on my birth certificate. When years later in the US I heard the song by Johnny Cash about "a boy named Sue," I chuckled with pride because I had fought many fights over my Chinese name.

It was past noon before Hung Tzer appeared. I soon discovered (mostly from snitches of gossip I overheard around the house) that she gambled until all hours of the morning, either playing *mahjong* at home or frequenting the casinos in Macao. This was by no means unusual for Hong Kong residents.

Gambling in China goes as far back as 2000 B.C. It is largely a social behavior thoroughly ingrained in Chinese culture. Hong Kong has always been a gambler's paradise. *Mahjong* is played everywhere with friends and relatives, for fun and relaxation—this social gambling is ignored by the government as long as it is not carried out as a public business. With increasing prosperity, making money has become an important motive. This wealth encourages greater risk taking which in turn leads to increased gambling. Another influence is superstition and belief in luck (not probability—that is, assessing the odds of winning).

Gambling in Hong Kong is strictly regulated and limited

to the Mark Six Lottery and betting on horse races at two racetracks (and more recently also on soccer) through non-profit services. Casinos are strictly prohibited. Thus many Hong Kong residents gamble in the casinos of Macao, today a 30-minute jet-boat ride from Hong Kong. Or they use illegal bookies or gamble at offshore sites via the Internet. The Hong Kong government has now outlawed online gambling (except through the Jockey Club) because it substantially cut into their revenue from other forms of gambling.

A Study of Hong Kong People's Participation in Gambling Activities (2001) found that "almost four out of five respondents had participated in at least one of the thirteen gambling activities listed. About half were involved in social gambling (*mahjong* and cards). A large proportion of pathological gamblers learned their skills from family at a young age."

I found out later that Hung Tzer's husband was part owner of a casino in Macao. He also owned several buildings on Nathan Road, as well as two jewelry stores. He was in his fifties, and Hung Tzer was in her early thirties. I thought she was stunningly beautiful. She had three children, a twelve year old son and two rather brash daughters, ten and eight.

Hung Tzer, her children, and her servants lived on the second floor of this building. The rooms seemed to me enormous and luxurious, with wall hangings and expensive mahogany furniture everywhere. Large Chinese vases, many of them empty, stood in every corner. And each bedroom had a gleaming spittoon. Hung Tzer was wife number four but apparently the favorite because the husband slept with her every night. Hung Tzer gave me one of the large guest rooms and occasionally some pocket money—she was very good to me.

The first floor was occupied by two guards, two servants and three children brought home by Hung Tzer's husband who had fathered them in past relationships. The third floor belonged to the third wife with one daughter and one son and servants. The fourth floor belonged to wife number two with one child, a son. During my stay I saw her only once as she was in poor health and was always coughing.

Wife number one, who was the only wife officially recognized by the British government, lived on the top floor. The others were all married in a Chinese ceremony, but were considered to be concubines by the Colony's officials. Wife number one was rather portly, with short hair and a jarring voice. She had one son and one daughter. The son was in his late twenties but still lived at home. The daughter was studying at a University in England. I did not like wife number one and her son because they treated me like a servant.

Three of the wives (excluding wife number two) frequently got together with a female friend and played *mahjong* for hours. The stakes were presumably very high. I was not allowed to be in the room.

As soon as I could, I went to look for Father Des. I took the Star Ferry to Hong Kong Island and found his office there. After I handed Father Peter's letter to the receptionist, Father Des appeared and gave me a big hug. I thought he resembled my own father, being skinny with a big nose (compared to mine, anyway).

Father Des immediately put me to work. Since my French at that time was better than my English, he spoke with me in French. He told me there was much filing to be done and I could help him communicate with the Chinese receptionist because he had trouble understanding her. His Cantonese truly was atrocious, whereas I spoke the dialect fluently. Other chores would be wiping chairs, tables and windows, dumping garbage, and running errands. He also mentioned a Catholic school nearby I should plan to attend while continuing to work after school.

School started in mid-September. By this time, some things happened in Hung Tzer's household that made me uncomfortable and renewed my desire to find a way to leave for America. First of all, the guard at the gate seemed reluctant to let me in and out—it was a constant hassle.

Then I was asked to help Hung Tzer's three children with their English. My own English was poor—learned in the Jesuit schools, not from my father who had only spoken Cantonese and some Mandarin at home. I didn't think I was able to do a good job tutoring, although I was glad there was something that I could do to contribute.

One day I accidentally walked into one of the family's rooms and found Hung Tzer sitting cross-legged on a big bed, where her husband was lounging with what I recognized was an opium pipe. While she was heating some opium paste on a pin over a large candle flame inside a bulbous glass jar, she asked me, "What do you want?"

I proudly answered, "I'm now going to school…"

Hung Tzer sternly interrupted me, "We will talk about this later. Right now, leave this room! Do not say anything to anyone about what you have just seen!"

As I walked out rather shaken, I became aware of the sickly sweet smell in the room, and I noticed that Hung Tzer had stuck the roasted substance into a hole at one end of her husband's pipe which he then placed over the flame, taking one big puff.

Two days later, one of the older *goong yan* came to my room. She informed me, "You will now be staying with me."

Then she packed up what little possessions I had. She had a bunk bed, and I was given the top bunk. Her room was so small that my few belongings could barely be crammed into a corner. The servants' quarters were quite a come-down from the chic lodgings I had enjoyed before.

When I saw Hung Tzer later, she did not volunteer the reason why I was banished to the servants' quarters. I eventually came up with a plausible explanation: I had told her after the bedroom incident that I had started school, was working afternoons, and Father Des had taken care of my tuition. I thought this news would make her happy. However, she may have felt the temporary guest wanted to become a permanent part of the family—hence, putting me in the servants' quarters would let me know I had worn out my welcome and should leave. This was confirmed years later by my cousin Ho Siu Hwa.

In addition to these incentives for leaving, I now had an American passport obtained at the US Consulate in Hong Kong. I was told by a consular official that the condition of being issued this passport (shown on the next page) was that I would have to swear an oath of allegiance to the United States at age 21—that was the law of the land. Then I could be issued a certificate of citizenship.

I turned fifteen at the end of September. My birthday went largely unobserved, although Father Des gave me two August moon cakes—a sweet treat I still relish. In my family, children's birthdays were rarely mentioned, nor celebrated. My mother used to comment that birthday presents for children were inappropriate because childbearing was painful and hard work—thus a child's birthday should be a time for thanking and honoring the mother.

Hong Kong Interlude: A Way to America

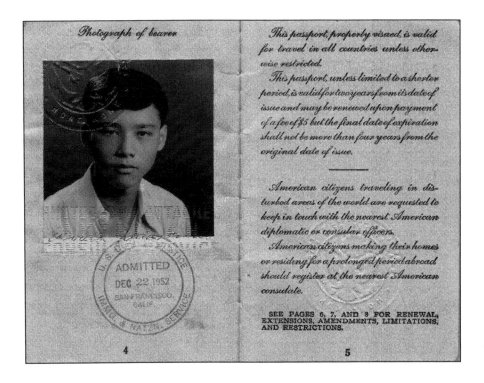

I knew several families in Hong Kong that had come from Shanghai. The Gaans in particular were very friendly toward me. The two daughters, fifteen and seventeen, were beautiful with blue eyes and black hair. Occasionally, I was invited to have dinner with them. I was always very impressed that they prayed before the meal. The father was a banker and took a special interest in my welfare.

One evening I talked with the family about my need to earn enough money to go to America. To my astonishment, they immediately held hands and prayed for me, asking God specifically to find a way for me to get to the US. Up to that point my experience with prayer had been limited to reciting numerous Our Father and Hail Mary prayers after confession. I believed common people could only say the prescribed prayers in church, and I saw prayer being mainly the responsibility of priests.

Mr. Gaan offered a suggestion, "Since merchant ships are coming into Hong Kong harbor all the time and since you are now fifteen, you might get a job on one of the ships." He then gave me the names of several shipping firms.

A few days later, I ate with the family again. They asked, "Did you try to get a job on board one of the ships?"

I shook my head. They didn't ask me why not but prayed again.

That evening I confessed to the two daughters, "I don't know how to go about getting such a job."

They opened the newspaper and wrote down several ships coming into Hong Kong or in the harbor already. One was the *Anna Mærsk*. "We don't know if this ship will go to America. It belongs to the A.P. Møller Shipping Company, a large Danish firm with many ships that frequently come to Hong Kong." This sounded promising.

Thus the next day I hired a motorized sampan (water taxi) to take me to the *Anna Mærsk* anchored out in Victoria Harbor. The ship was surrounded by many small boats. I did not really pay any attention to them but looked up at the tall blue hull and even taller masts and booms. I noticed several crewmen standing on planks suspended half-way up—it looked as if they were painting. The sampan dropped me off at a platform, from where I was able to climb a wobbly stairway made of small planks and ropes to get on board. The scene was chaotic, with cargo being loaded with the on-board booms.

I approached one of the persons on deck who was Caucasian and who seemed to have some authority. Summoning my courage, I asked, "Please. Could I see someone who could hire me?" He turned and gruffly ordered one of the

Hong Kong Interlude: A Way to America

seamen standing nearby to fetch the chief steward.

When the chief steward appeared, he said, "We are short a pantry boy." Then he took me to see the captain.

The captain informed us, "We have already requested Denmark to send a boy."

"I can work hard," I pleaded in broken English.

"Why do you want a job on my ship?"

I stuttered, "I want to work ... my way to the United States." Proudly, I showed him my American passport.

"The *Anna Mærsk* only sails around the Far East," the captain told me, "but the *Laura Mærsk* will be coming into port in a few days—she sails between the Far East and the United States."

"Would there be ... job for me ... on the *Laura Mærsk*?"

The captain replied, "I don't know."

With my limited English, I began to argue, saying something along the lines that if he hired me, I could later transfer to a Mærsk ship going to the US.

In dismissal, the captain said, "This would be difficult to do; your best chance is to hire on with a ship that sails to the United States."

My shoulders drooped and I left.

Some days after my failed interview, the *Laura Mærsk* came into Victoria Harbor. The next afternoon, I took a sampan to go out to the ship anchored at buoy. This time I immediately asked for the chief steward and was taken to his cabin. He had the typical Scandinavian look, with red hair and blue eyes. His English was fluent, and he also spoke French.

The steward was fascinated to see a young Chinese boy who spoke French and some English. I was thrilled when he told me, "Our cabin boy jumped ship in Bangkok—he didn't show up when the ship sailed from its last port. So, we are in need of a cabin boy."

My hopes were immediately dashed when the steward continued, "It is customary for us to send for a boy from Denmark." But I perked up some upon hearing, "We should go and see the master of the ship—the captain."

The captain was not in his office when we knocked. We found him on the far side of the bridge, talking to the chief engineer. When I first saw him, he did not fit my image of a captain. The captain of the *Anna Mærsk* had looked very much like the image I had formed of captains from watching Hollywood movies. But the captain of the *Laura Mærsk* had a fluffy mane of white hair, was slightly hunch-backed, and wore a plain shirt instead of a uniform jacket.

Waving us into his office next to the bridge, he only spoke with the chief steward. After talking in Danish with the captain for about five minutes, the chief steward asked for my US passport and passed it on to the captain. After the document was returned to me, they continued in Danish for a few minutes.

Then the chief steward motioned for me to follow him out of the office. I politely bowed and extended my hand to the captain to thank him for seeing me. He shook my hand but did not smile nor did he say a word. I had the sinking feeling the chief steward was going to tell me I did not get the job.

As we came down from the ship's bridge to the main deck, the chief steward put his arm around my shoulder and said words in formal French that I will never forget, *"Mon garçon, vous travaillerez pour moi* (My boy, you will be working for me)."

He then took me over to the first mate who signed me

up as *hovmestermedhjælper*. Although the official Danish document translated this as mess man, the position in essence was cabin boy.

After this, the chief steward showed me my quarters and introduced me to the other boys with whom I would share the cabin: the pantry boy, the baker's helper, and the mess boy. The cabin had two double bunks, a small table in the center, as well as a sofa against one wall and four compartments on the opposite wall where we could stow our belongings. The chief steward apologized for its being so cramped and added I would get used to it. I thought it looked comfortable compared to the attic I had slept in when growing up in Shanghai.

The chief steward explained that in two days the ship would leave early in the morning for Saigon, French Indochina. Thus I should go ashore and say goodbye to my family and friends and bring my belongings on board by next evening at the latest. I was expected to start work as soon as the ship left the harbor and would be paid starting that day (which, according to my records, was October 24, 1952). The pay was the equivalent of one US dollar per day in Danish kroners (Dkr). Each payday the first mate would write in each seaman's ledger the amount of money earned, and we would be allowed to draw out money in local currency when docked in port.

I went back to Hung Tzer's place and quickly packed. Although it was getting late, I then rushed to my cousin Ho Siu Hwa and exuberantly spilled out my news, "I got a job on a ship going to America!"

"I'm so happy for you," she beamed. Her husband James kept putting up his thumbs and repeated, *"Ho one"* (which means good luck or good fortune).

My cousin asked me for a favor, "Could you please bring James to meet Father Des before you leave?" James was still unemployed since the day they had come to Hong Kong. He stayed home and cared for their newborn son—an unusual situation in those days and culture, to say the least.

I then took a cab over to the Gaans. The girls were jumping with joy at the news. The father told me he was delighted God had answered their prayers, and he asked me to pray with him to thank God. I was quite surprised to see this otherwise intelligent man would think God Almighty would spend that much time taking care of such an insignificant petition. A quick thought ran through my mind—if all 800 million Chinese prayed for different things, God would run out of time to do more important matters like creating more worlds.

However, I did not pursue this thought, but went back to telling the girls in much detail about what had happened that day, greatly exaggerating my salesmanship in convincing the captain to hire me. As I was leaving, the girls kissed me and said in Mandarin *"tsai gee-an"* (which means "see you again" since there is no literal expression for goodbye in Chinese). The mother hugged me. The father shook my hand with both of his around mine while saying, "God go with you, my boy" and repeating this in Spanish, *"Vaya con Dios, mi muchacho."*

Early the next day I went with James to see Father Des. After I told Father Des the news, he hugged and squeezed me so hard I thought all the air from my lungs was expelled. I introduced James and explained the reason I had brought him. Father Des said because James had a degree in Chinese literature and spoke English, he might be able to teach at the

Catholic school I had attended. Father Des then wrote a note for the headmaster of the school.

James and I immediately walked over to the school, and while James talked to the headmaster, I went to say my farewells to the three Jesuit Brothers I knew from Shanghai—Brother Jacob, Brother Kevin, and Brother Jimboom. Jimboom was a nickname, and all the students called him that, but he did not mind. He was credited with having magical powers, and each time he used his head on a soccer ball, it made a startling "boom" sound. The only photo I have from my days at St. Joan of Arc (described in Chapter 3) shows Brother Jimboom in the midst of my classmates.

On leaving the Catholic school, James thanked me for helping him. He took me to a restaurant for dim sum—dumplings and other small dishes selected from carts and trays brought to the table by waiters. Then he accompanied me to Hung Tzer's place.

While waiting for her to return from shopping, I went all over the building explaining to everyone willing to listen that I was leaving as soon as I had a chance to say farewell to Hung Tzer—I had not taken time earlier to tell anyone there about my job on the ship. At the top floor, wife number one wished me luck in Cantonese. But her son muttered goodbye in English with a look that clearly meant, "Good riddance to a piece of rubbish" while waving impatiently for me to go. This was my only sad moment during the last two days.

I started to pace to and fro and getting more and more agitated and impatient—I didn't want to be late in getting to the ship. It was almost dark by the time Hung Tzer finally appeared. After hearing my news, she gave me a big smile and asked me to wait for a minute. She went into her bedroom and shortly came out with one of the traditional red envelopes with money that are handed out in China on special occasions for good luck. I said goodbye to her children and the servants but did not see her husband. One of the older *goong yan* cried. With one small bag in hand, I left.

Three months earlier, I had felt abandoned upon arriving in Hong Kong. Now, I was ready to confidently face the unknown risks on my way toward achieving the American dream. With a swagger, I took a taxi and then a sampan and went on board the *Laura Mærsk*. Cargo was still being loaded with the on-board booms from the junk boats moored alongside the ship. From the main deck I walked over to my cabin, pushed the small bag into my storage compartment, took off my shoes and socks, and climbed onto my bunk. Without saying one word to the pantry boy, I fell into a deep sleep.

7
Life on a Tramp Ship

The next morning, I abruptly woke when pulled by the blanket to the floor. The bully was the muscular pantry boy, Kierkegaard Jørgensen, who stood glaring down at me. He had the typical Nordic look with blond hair and blue eyes. In heavy accented English, he sneered, "Time to get up." The other two boys—the baker's helper and the mess boy—were up and dressed already.

I scrambled to my feet. Kierkegaard took me to the bathroom. He growled, *"Du stinke,"* holding his nose to emphasize his point. Then he motioned for me to take a shower and left. After I gave myself a good scrub and dressed, I went on deck and saw the ship had begun to move. As I was watching the Chinese sampans receding, feelings of relief mixed with happiness rushed over me, and I could hardly keep from shouting, "I am no longer one of them—I am going to America, to become a real American!"

At that moment, the boatswain pointed to me and yelled something in Danish. Two seamen rushed towards me and I fully expected them to throw me overboard. They drew up short when the captain bellowed through a bullhorn from the bridge. I was relieved when the chief steward appeared and explained, "The boatswain thought you were a stowaway, since you have not yet been introduced to him."

The chief steward took me on a tour of the living quarters amidships while he explained the responsibilities of a cabin boy or *kabine dreng*. "Your job is to daily vacuum the officers' cabins (all seven) as well as mine and the radio officer's, except Sundays. Dirty towels need to be taken to the laundry room. Make up the beds daily and change the sheets weekly or when requested. And empty the waste paper baskets." As we passed through a hallway, he continued, "You also have to clean the hallways and twice weekly polish all the brass portholes and brass railings amidships. And whenever the chief mate or I ask, you will serve us coffee and other refreshments."

At this point, the chief steward let me go on deck so I could watch the ship leave Victoria Harbor. I saw Kowloon to the northeast, surrounded by the New Territories to the north. To the west was Lantau Island, with Hong Kong Island to the southeast. Then the ship turned south into the Lamma Channel. The pilot we had taken on board to guide the *Laura Mærsk* out of the harbor soon left on a small motor boat. The ship moved steadily into the South China Sea. Hong Kong Island with Victoria Peak at its center was slowly disappearing behind us.

As I was admiring the changing scenery, the chief steward approached, holding a camera. I was very self-conscious because of my shabby clothes and begged, "Please don't take my picture." But he insisted that I pose. He then had to take two snapshots, because I had put my hands over my face in the first one.

Life on a Tramp Ship

"It's time to eat and then get to work—you only have a half-hour for lunch." The chief steward escorted me to the steamy galley where the cook and baker were busy cleaning up after preparing lunch for the entire crew and passengers. The cook did not speak English but later became my best friend on board.

When the chief steward said that my name was Edward, the cook laughed, pointed at me, and exclaimed, "Hans!"

I was astonished when the chief steward responded in French, *"Votre nom est maintenant Hans* (your name is now Hans)"—he had no way of knowing that Hans, which is John in English, was my baptism name.

From then on, everyone on board called me Hans except Kierkegaard who called me *gul sazan* or *gul djaevel*, both meaning "yellow devil." He never called me Hans, with one surprising exception at the end of our relationship. When within earshot of one of the officers, he would be more polite by calling me *kinesisk dreng* (Chinese boy).

I quickly learned the difference between *du* and *de*. Kierkegaard used commands like *du komme* a lot, and it did not take long for me to realize that *du* meant "you." In English or Chinese there is only one form for this pronoun, and I was not yet aware that Danish was like French which differentiates between the familiar and the polite forms. After I had learned a little Danish, I used the pronoun *du* with an officer who—normally a nice, easy-going person—went ballistic on me and chewed me out. From then on, when in doubt, I used the formal *de*.

Everyone on board was Danish except for two Norwegians (the second officer and one seaman) and a Finnish stoker (or oiler). All officers spoke English, some fluently.

The Norwegians and Danes had no trouble understanding each other, but the Finn, who spoke little English or Danish, had a hard time. The chief steward was multilingual; the first waiter spoke fluent English, and the second waiter spoke some English. Since neither the baker, nor the cook, nor the boys spoke more than a few words of English, I quickly had to learn Danish to get along.

It took me a little while to discover the chain of command on the ship. The officers serving directly under the captain were the chief mate, two deck officers (mates), the radio officer, four engineers (including the chief engineer) and the chief steward. The crewmembers normally consisted of the boatswain who was in charge of all the seamen which included six able-bodied seamen, three junior able-bodied seamen, one deck boy, four stokers, one carpenter, two engine assistants, and one apprentice. In addition, there were a coxswain, one cook, one baker, two waiters, a cook's helper, and four cabin boys, for a total of thirty-nine persons who manned the ship.

The deck boy stayed astern with the seamen, but the cabin boys were housed right behind the fourth engineer's cabin amidships. Although we were a tramp merchant ship, we could take on a maximum of twelve passengers. The chief steward was in charge of the cabin boys, waiters, baker, cook, and cook's helper. His priority was looking to the comfort of the captain and passengers.

The engineers were responsible for the engine room. The mates saw to it that the ship ran on course. They arranged for the loading and unloading of cargo and passengers, paid the crew, and had other duties for daily operations and keeping everything shipshape. The seamen took orders from the mates for running and steering the ship—they in essence took care of everything above the engine room. But the majority of the time they were busy chipping rust and painting the ship.

Specifications for the **Laura Mærsk**

Length 484 ft, width 59 ft, height (keel to top of masts) 122 ft. Speed (full load) 15.5 knots. Deadweight (dwt) 9,100 tons. Two decks, three steel masts, 23 derricks. Three anchors. Holds for grain and bales; refrigerated holds for perishables; tanks for water and fuel oil. Two 7-cylinder Burmeister & Wain diesel engines at 7,400 HP; two boilers; three 225 HP diesel engines coupled to 150 kW dynamos for winches & electrical equipment.

Launch: 2/1939, A.P. Møller's Odense Steelship Yards, Denmark. Cost: 4 Million Dkr. Sold in 12/1963 for 2 Million Dkr to Transfruit Shipping Co. Ltd., Athens, Greece. renamed Aeolion.

By now it was past one in the afternoon. The cook pointed to me while making a comment to the chief steward. He translated, "The cook wants me to remind you that lunch for the boys is provided between noon and one, but for your first day, he is making an exception."

This lunch was boiled cabbage, potatoes, a large sausage with a big dollop of mustard, and a Danish pastry from the baker. Before I had time to wonder where I should take my tray, the steward said, "You boys can eat on deck, in your room, in the lounge—a small cabin with four bar stools at a high counter—or sitting on the floor outside the galley." But I found we could only eat on deck when the sea was calm—otherwise the food would get drenched with salt spray.

After my first lunch on board, I began my rounds of vacuuming and making the beds. The sea was smooth, and the work was easy. That evening after my chores I went on deck and was treated to an unforgettable sight—a brilliant orange sunset mirrored in beautiful, calm waters as the ship sailed serenely across the South China Sea. I found that there was no rigid schedule, but bedtime was normally between nine and ten. I could get up around six or even seven, depending on the work that needed to be done.

The next day, the mess boy showed me how I could enjoy gourmet food like an officer. We would go into the officers' dining room after they had eaten. I helped him bus the tables, all the while gobbling down whatever leftovers appealed to me. I was partial to smorgasbord. I learned to really like pickled herring with onions and plenty of butter on black bread. I ate more potatoes in the time I spent on the ship than in my entire life before that. But we rarely had rice on board which I missed. I also drank lots of milk and grew over two inches as a result of this abundant fare.

It took three days to reach the mouth of the Mekong River on our way to Saigon. We picked up a pilot as well as a tall French foreign legionnaire who set up a machine gun at the stern of the ship as we steadily proceeded up the muddy Mekong. Both sides of the river were covered high with green elephant grass—a splendid sight. It took several hours before we reached the port of Saigon. We received extra pay for the days we were around Saigon. When I asked the chief steward about the legionnaire, he explained, "*Les Français ont combattu les Viet Mings depuis des années* (The French have been fighting the Viet Mings for years)."

From Saigon we sailed for two days and anchored off Kohsichang in Thailand. That evening, three or four seamen were on the gangplank using a sawed-off eggbeater at the end of a long pole to harpoon water moccasins. Under a bright light, I could see the water churning with what seemed to be hundreds of snakes. Kierkegaard explained to me that water snakes were not poisonous. However, I had already learned caution where he was concerned, so I kept my distance from the snakes. The seamen caught at least a dozen moccasins, some about four feet long and six inches in diameter—for the sport and the snake skins.

The cook (on the right in the photo, next to the cook's helper and the baker) told me later it was good I had stayed away because these *vander slangers* could be deadly.

The next day we sailed along the Gulf of Thailand for Bangkok and arrived there in a few hours. We stayed in Bangkok for five days, and for the first time I went ashore. The city reminded me very much of Hong Kong because of the hundreds of sampans (long-tail boats) on the Chao Pharaya River. On these boats, families lived and died, generation after generation. However, unlike in Hong Kong, these boats were also used for making a living by selling fruit and vegetables.

It was very hot as I toured Bangkok, and few places were air-conditioned. I mainly got around the city on the human-powered three-wheeler cycle that was like the pedicab in China. I was very much impressed by the majestic pagodas and splendid temples throughout the city.

From Bangkok it took five days to sail through the Gulf of Thailand and the South China Sea into the Sulu Sea to the city of Iloilo, the "Queen City of the South," which is at the center of the Philippine archipelago. There was no pier, so we had to anchor offshore. That evening the seamen were at it again with their bright lights and spearing of water snakes.

From Iloilo we sailed to Cebu; it took more than a day to travel a distance of less than a hundred miles. Countless islands dotted the horizon, and the ship was traveling at caution speed as the water was treacherous with many reefs. Whenever I could, I would come out on deck because the sea was like a sheet of smooth paper, with the bow of the ship slicing through it like a sharp knife. Flying fish would dart up and glide fifty or more feet before plopping back into the water. The scenery was truly breathtaking and simply overwhelmed me, having experienced little beyond crowded city life in Shanghai and Hong Kong.

From Cebu it took more than a day to sail to Manila on the Island of Luzon. It is the largest city in the Philippines, only a short distance south of Quezon City, the capital. We stayed one day to load and unload cargo "off anchored" in Manila Bay (as noted in the Captain's log). Then we sailed back to Hong Kong. As usual, we tied up to a buoy in Victoria Harbor. We were there only twenty-five hours.

I had permission to take the day off to go ashore. The Gaan family was happy to see me. The girls were delighted that I was tanned and looking fit and strong. They wanted to know everything that had happened to me in the short thirty days since my departure from Hong Kong, and they asked, "Are the Danes on board treating you well?" I described the ship, the beautiful scenery and the places I had seen. I did not tell them about my nemesis Kierkegaard Jørgensen. They insisted I stay for lunch, and again Mr. Gaan said a memorable prayer for me, thanking God for His guiding hand in my life. I was quite touched.

Already during this first voyage, I had learned a lot about the tramp trade, but I didn't get the full picture until recently, when I had the chance to read a biography of A.P. Møller, the founder of the shipping company. Now, more than sixty years later, the Danish Mærsk conglomerate does business in over 130 countries and is headquartered in Copenhagen. It operates the largest container ships and tankers, as well as drilling rigs, oil wells, shipyards, and even supermarkets.

On April 8, 2009, the 17,000-ton *Mærsk Alabama* was in the news when it was hijacked by Somali pirates while en route to Mombasa, Kenya. In 2013, the movie "Captain Phillips"—a thriller staring Tom Hanks—was based on the true story of this hijacking and became a box office success.

By 1956, no tramp steamers remained in the company, and the construction with the bridge, living quarters and engine room amidships (as seen on the motor ship *Laura*

Mærsk) was abandoned by 1957. On later cargo ships, engine room and accommodations were placed three-quarters or completely astern. The *Emma Mærsk* (launched in 2006) is one of the largest container ships with an astoundig capacity of 11,000 fourteen-ton containers. On this ship, quarters and bridge are placed about two-thirds astern. At 1302.5 ft, it was the longest ship afloat in 2007 (from Ove Hornby, *With Constant Care, A.P. Møller: Shipowner, 1876-1965*). Every time I see the blue seven-pointed Mærsk star on a truck along a highway, I get a warm feeling in my heart, as I gratefully remember my time at sea on one of their ships.

8
Voyage to "New Gold Mountain"

My brief shore leave in Hong Kong included a visit to Father Des and the school where my cousin Ho Siu Hwa's husband James had just started to teach. Also, I stopped by to see Hung Tzer. The first question she asked was, "How much do you make?" Then she ordered one of the servants to immediately start cooking for an early dinner; she took it for granted I would stay for the meal.

I was relieved when we set sail the next morning for Keelung, Formosa (now Taiwan). As we entered the Formosa Straits heading north and slightly east, the sea was very rough. The ship was tilting—portside to starboard, portside to starboard—in continual, never-ending motion, even though there was no storm. I learned later this stretch of sea is rough nearly year round. I became very seasick and almost puked in the first mate's cabin. I left the vacuum cleaner in the cabin and bracing myself against the walls staggered to my room and climbed onto my bunk. For the first time in my life I wanted to die—it seemed preferable to being seasick. I felt as sick doubled up in bed as when standing, and I was utterly unable to work.

After twenty minutes or so, the chief steward came into my cabin and joked, "Are you trying to get out of work? It must be your Chinese blood, because Danes don't get seasick." He then got Kierkegaard to finish my job.

That evening I was still seasick. Kierkegaard came into the cabin and yelled at me in Danish. His body language told me he was not wishing me well. To my surprise, I could make out many words he repeated during the tirade, such as *kinesisk lus* (Chinese louse) punctuated by *dum, stum* and *stinke*, all of which were easy to understand in or out of context. A word he used several times was *doven*, which I was to find out eventually meant "lazy." To his credit, I don't remember him ever using profanity.

After two days, we approached Keelung at the northernmost tip of the island of Formosa. As we passed the jetty coming into port, we finally found calm water. Right away, I began to feel better. Most of the Keelung dock area was filled with large booms the Japanese had built during World War Two and then left behind when they surrendered. Thus we did not need to use our ship's booms as was done in Hong Kong or anywhere else we anchored at buoy. Many of the seamen and a few officers went ashore shortly after the ship docked, but all the boys stayed on board. I did not see any point in going ashore since this was still China in my mind, and I wanted to get away from it.

The morning after we docked in Keelung, I was very hungry. The cook, using sign language, indicated he wanted to prepare a special breakfast for me because I had thrown up everything the previous two days. When I handed him my plate, he gave me two sunny-side-up eggs, a piece of beef, a large potato, beans, and toast. I took that into the cabin with the bar stools. I had never seen sunny-side-up eggs in my life—in China we always ate eggs scrambled or fried on both sides.

Just then, Kierkegaard came into the room with a plate that had only one egg, a potato, beans, and toast. When I cut up my potato and eggs and mixed everything with the beans, he started to shout at me with his usual vocabulary of

Voyage to "New Gold Mountain"

"stupid, dumb Chinese" and similar deprecating words. The photo shows a grinning Kierkegaard with the mess boy.

He smacked me over the head and motioned for me to see how sunny-side-up eggs were to be eaten. He slowly cut his egg around the yolk. Then laying down the knife, he switched hands from left to right to hold the fork. He balanced the yolk on the fork without breaking it and shoved it into his mouth. Next, he ate the pieces of egg white. What an idiotic way to eat an egg, I thought, since the yolk could be hot and burn the tongue. Besides, I was perfectly comfortable gripping my fork with the left hand. Thus I decided to ignore him. The mess boy, who had been in the cabin, came over on his way out and told Kierkegaard something in Danish—I guessed it was to let me eat however I wanted. Kierkegaard shot back with a word I came to learn was "shut-up." Kierkegaard somehow made me feel ashamed I was Chinese.

I discovered later that I was born left-handed but was forced by my mother—with more than a few raps on the knuckles—to use the right hand for writing and eating with chopsticks. In the Chinese culture at that time, being left-handed was thought to bring bad luck. But from then on, when eating Western style, I always used the left hand to hold the fork. Even today, when I am with companions in a tight eating space, I'm careful to pick my seat so I will not interfere with other people's arms holding either forks or chopsticks. This especially applies to airplane seating.

From Keelung we headed east into the Pacific Ocean and then sailed north for four days to Yokohama, a seaport south of Tokyo. We then zigzagged to different ports in the southern part of Japan: Kobe, Nagoya, and finally Shimizu. These short trips took about one day each and we would dock for less than a day, each time to load and unload cargo. I did not go ashore at any of the ports in Japan. I rationally knew the people who had conducted the war were not the same people who came on board to load and unload. Also, the war had been over for seven years—yet I still harbored mixed emotions of fear and hatred as I watched the Japanese dockworkers go about their ordinary business.

From Shimizu we started to sail east across the Pacific, heading toward Vancouver, Canada, a voyage taking fifteen days. About six days out, we met with a fierce storm—a typhoon. The ship was tossed about like a log caught in a tide. When a giant wave nearly lifted the entire ship out of the water, I heard the propellers spinning in the air. Then the ship sank back into a deep valley, with a wall of water rushing over the entire ship. We traveled at a snail's pace.

The storm lasted nearly a day and a half. Curiously, I did not get seasick in this storm, nor during any other rough seas for the entire time I remained on the ship. I got a glimpse of the captain who looked very pale. In the galley I noticed many pots and pans swinging like pendulums, with dishes sliding back and forth on the counters. Although the cook and baker kept preparing meals, most passengers and a few crewmembers did not have much of an appetite. I was intrigued that the dishes served to the passengers and officers were placed on devices that kept them horizontal no matter which way the ship was tilting.

About ten days out from Japan, in the middle of the Pacific, the sailors started to get rowdy. It was customary to relieve the tedium as well as tempers halfway through a long ocean crossing by having boxing matches between those that had some grievances. After two seamen had enough of punching each other around, the cook handed a pair of boxing gloves to me and another pair to Kierkegaard on the opposite side of the crowd.

Then the cook came around and patted me on the back. Pointing to Kierkegaard, he said, "Hans, *sla ham*." He meant for me to hit him or beat him.

"*Nej*," I said, shaking my head.

But when Kierkegaard started cackling to taunt me, I took the gloves. I had been a scrappy kid in Shanghai, always in a fight, so this was not new to me. Kierkegaard grinned when he put on his gloves—he was three years older, well built, and much heavier than I. His mocking glances told me he would like nothing better than to knock me off the ship. I was angry—in fact, hate is not too strong a word for my feelings towards him, engendered by his constant bullying. He began to punch me while I mostly tried to protect my face. Then he hit me full in the stomach. That really hurt since I was very scrawny.

The cook yelled excitedly, "Hans, *dræbe*"—I understood that he said for me to "kill him."

To my astonishment, the crowd started to chant, "Hans, Hans, Hans"—I hadn't realized the crew was on my side since I had assumed most of them to be prejudiced except for the cook (and the captain, of course). With a rush of adrenaline and my head down, I moved towards Kierkegaard like a torpedo and struck him. He stumbled and let his arms fall momentarily. In a flash, I punched him with my left glove so ferociously that I almost blacked out. But I connected well and decked him.

While he was still stretched out, I continued to punch him everywhere I found an open spot, especially in the groin area—in the streets of Shanghai we were used to keep hitting when our opponents were down. I think I was just about ready to really kill him when three seamen pulled me up and said, "Okay, *stoppe*."

From that day on, Kierkegaard never smacked me around again, although he still called me *kinesisk dreng* and *gul sazan*.

A few days later, Captain Lindberg asked the chief steward to move me into the pilot's cabin, which was on the bridge. It was rarely used except as a washroom for the pilot during the short time when one was on board. I cannot remember any pilot being put up overnight. I'm guessing the captain heard about my fight with Kierkegaard from one of the officers and decided to put some distance between us. The captain also gave me some of his clothes and shoes since I only had one pair of shoes and one pair of sandals. In the photo above, I'm at ease in clean and

Voyage to "New Gold Mountain"

pressed clothing.

Although I always worked very hard—Kierkegaard thought me a sycophant—neither the chief steward nor the captain ever complimented me on my good work. However, on more than one occasion, when I was polishing brass on deck, Captain Lindberg would look down from the bridge with a smile and give me a friendly wave. That used to cheer me more than he could ever imagine. It also meant a lot to me when one of the seamen trusted me—though only for the span of a half hour—to actually steer the ship under his watchful eye.

On December 18, we docked in Vancouver and then left the following day for San Francisco. We arrived there on December 22, 1952, as shown by a stamp in my passport. I called my brother Charlie, and he came on board to fetch me. He informed me that he now had an American nickname: Chuck. I was able to get three days off to be with him and our father, spending Christmas Eve with them. They lived in a one-room efficiency apartment. I slept in my cabin on the ship at night, because their apartment was too small for an extra sleeper. The docking area in the cold and gloom of the day gave me the impression of a graveyard with its bleak rails and cranes.

Chuck was going to school and worked evenings as an usher in a theatre. My father had found and then lost two good jobs because of accusations of being a Communist sympathizer. This was a different picture of "Old Gold Mountain" from what I had dreamed about, and I realized I did not want to stay here. Instead, I withdrew all the money I had in my ship account and gave it to Chuck to send to our mother in Shanghai.

I have only recently discovered that my father had worked as a crew messman on the *S.S. Oregonian* when he was nineteen, sailing from San Francisco to New York and back (from November 1928 to January 1929). He got sick on the way back and ended up in the Marine Corps Hospital in San Francisco for several months. It puzzles and saddens me why he never mentioned this experience to me.

On December 26 we set sail for Los Angeles, arriving there the next day. Three days later we were heading south toward the Panama Canal and thus spent New Year's Day sailing along the Mexican coast. On New Year's Eve, the seamen had been allowed an extra beer to the allotted daily two by order of the captain. But some had managed to smuggle beer on board, and quite a few seamen got drunk.

Most of the crewmembers were smoking, and thus at fifteen I started smoking as well. All the boys smoked, except Kierkegaard. Two packs a day were provided on board at an extremely low price.

We arrived in the Canal Zone in Panama and docked at the city of Balboa on January 6, 1953. Two days later, we headed into the Panama Canal. It connects the Pacific with the Atlantic Ocean and in those days was called the world's greatest shortcut—traversing through the Canal shortened the sea journey from New York to San Francisco by over 8400 miles. Each transit employs six immense locks that are true marvels of engineering, where each lock has a side-by-side double to let ship traffic go up or down independently.

The journey through the entire length of the Panama Canal was simply incredible in its contrast to the slums of Shanghai. I kept my eyes wide open and my brain in a state of total engagement and utter astonishment, both at the exquisite scenery and the technical achievement. I truly believe this experience lead towards my later becoming an engineer.

We sailed up the Atlantic seaboard to New York in six days and anchored in Brooklyn. Our next port was Philadelphia, and it took nearly twenty hours to round Cape May and sail up the Delaware. Then we continued south to Baltimore, which took almost two days as we had to round the Delmarva Peninsula and then go up the Chesapeake. From there we backtracked to Norfolk, Virginia, where we were in dry dock for eight days. The wintertime landscape did not look inviting, and thus I did not feel like sightseeing. The ship sailed back up to New York, arriving in Brooklyn on February 12, 1953. Then the *Laura Mærsk* stayed in New York for more than one month for crew changes and repairs.

Several crew changes affected me directly. Captain Lindberg retired, and Captain Obel came on board. This new captain was nothing like the grandfatherly figure Captain Lindberg had been to me. He was very formal and much younger than Captain Lindberg, perhaps in his late forties. However, he was never unkind to me.

Before Captain Lindberg left, he did one more thing for me for which I was very grateful: he promoted me to second waiter. I had been disappointed not to get the deck boy's position after he jumped ship in Balboa—the boatswain chose a boy who would spend his whole life at sea. Instead, I became, at fifteen, the youngest second waiter in the Mærsk Line at that time.

The following two pages show a map of the western and eastern Pacific, tracing my first two voyages on the *Laura Mærsk*. Not shown is the Pacific midsection extending from Kamchatka to Alaska and the Aleutian Islands. The distance from Shimizu to Vancouver is over 5000 miles. The indicated routes of the ship are my approximations.

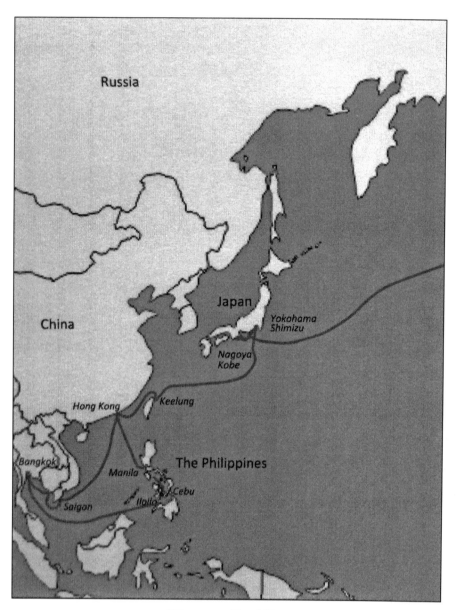

Western Pacific

The *Laura Mærsk* on my first journey sailed around the Far East from Hong Kong to Saigon, Bangkok, the Philippines and back to Hong Kong. Next we went to Taiwan and Japan.

Voyage to "New Gold Mountain"

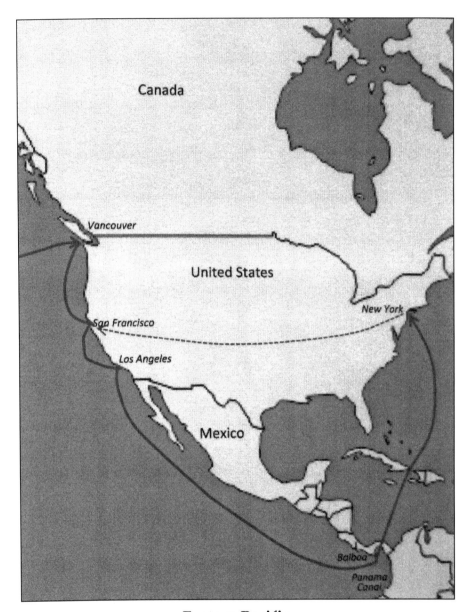

Eastern Pacific

From Japan, we crossed the Pacific to Vancouver, Canada, where we turned south to California and the Panama Canal, then north along the US coast to "New Gold Mountain."

I was sorry to see the chief steward return to Denmark. He had always treated me well, speaking to me in English or French and also teaching me Danish words that helped me do my assigned tasks better.

A new chief steward took over. He was an older version of Kierkegaard, except nastier: he smoked incessantly, drank heavily, and freely used profanity. He did not call me Hans but *kinesisk dreng.* Also during the crew changes, two new boys came on, one for my old position and one for the job vacated by the fellow promoted to deck boy.

Although I now had reached "New Gold Mountain," I didn't feel I wanted to live here. Like San Francisco at Christmas, this cold, forbidding city of New York was not the America of my dreams either. The ship by now had become my home—I had friends on board, and most of the others seemed to like me. Also, being the second waiter was a good job with the promise of further adventures.

However, I had a lump on the back of my head that was growing rapidly, and I asked the chief mate if I could get it looked at by a doctor. He directed me to the physician the Mærsk Line used in New York and said the company would pay for the costs of the visit as well as the taxi. After the doctor examined me, he indicated he would operate in his office the next day to remove what he diagnosed was a cyst. But after he cut open the cyst, he stitched it up again quickly and called an ambulance to take me to the United States Public Health Service Hospital on Staten Island. Mostly, US naval and merchant marine personnel used this hospital. I was admitted for tests and surgery. On that date, March 12, 1953, I was discharged from the *Laura Mærsk*.

While I waited in the hospital for the pathology report

on my cyst, the *Laura Mærsk* set sail on March 16. I was in a ward with two cancer patients. The word *cancer* got bounced around, and I somehow gained the impression that it was a common illness and nothing to fear, unless you were very old. In far-off Shanghai and then isolated on the ship, I had never heard of this disease and what it truly entailed—in those days, it was rarely talked about openly since it was considered to be the equivalent of a death sentence, and thus I had no clue.

I sent a telegram to my brother Chuck in San Francisco and to the Gaans in Hong Kong, notifying them that I was in the hospital on Staten Island with cancer. My brother wired back, asking for a progress report—he was unable to come to Staten Island because of the costs. The Gaans immediately cabled that they were praying for me and that friends of theirs, the Newell family from Baltimore, would come by to visit me.

When this family received the telegram from the Gaans, Mr. Newell, a lawyer, took a day off from work and drove with his family to see me. After introducing his wife and two children, he left to meet with the head of the team of doctors that had examined me. I didn't see why I should be fussed over—I felt that with an operation and some rest, I would soon be out of the hospital.

When Mr. Newell returned, he said the doctors did not think I had cancer, but that I was scheduled for surgery in a few days. Mr. Newell did not seem to be relieved but rather annoyed. I sensed he felt I had sent the telegram to the Gaans merely to gain attention. Soon after this, I learned the facts about cancer from a Danish seaman who was a patient in the same hospital.

Before my surgery, a perky lady from the A.P. Møller

Steamship Company came to see how I was doing. Although I think she would have known how to speak English, she only spoke in Danish with me. She expressed surprise to find a Chinese boy who spoke some Danish. I repeated to her several times, "*Jeg haver ing kræft* (I have no cancer)." She advised me to take all the time I needed to recuperate, and she assured me that the Company would cover all expenses. The best news of all was that I could either meet up with the ship in Panama or in San Francisco—they would arrange for the flight to either city.

After surgery to remove my epidermal cyst and several days of recovery, I was tested once more before I could be discharged the next day. The hospital must have informed the Steamship Company that I was ready to be released, since the lady, who visited me before, stopped by to give me more information.

She started by asking me, "Would you like to fly to San Francisco tomorrow to meet up with your ship there?"

When I nodded, she continued, "One of our employees will come and take you to the airport. And he will give you the airplane ticket then."

I beamed, "This is great news; thank you very much. I am eager to start my new job as second waiter."

Around noon I telephoned the Newells. Mr. Newell came after a while to take me to their house for dinner. I did not know that lawyers were wealthy, so seeing their large, stately home was a surprising revelation. They had two daughters; both very good looking, as were Mr. and Mrs. Newell. I have to confess that I envied this family—for a while I wished I could have had an American family like them. During the entire visit, I felt rather out of place, coupled with a good measure of curiosity in being for the first time in a real American home. The Newells had another dinner guest, I presume a lawyer colleague, who then took me back to the hospital. This was a three-hour ride in his chauffeur-driven car.

I was discharged from the hospital on April 7, 1953. Early that morning an employee of A.P. Møller Steamship Company picked me up and took me to the airport. He accompanied me to the gate, making sure I got on the plane OK. I had only one small bag. Boarding an airplane was a very simple procedure in those days, and passengers were seen off by family and friends right at the gate. My TWA plane was a four-engine DC-7 propeller aircraft. This was the first time that I would be flying on an airplane, and I was rather apprehensive. I think the plane made two stops; I do not remember having to change aircraft. The flight was uneventful and smooth, but I was still nervous for most of the way. The total time from New York to San Francisco was about twelve hours, leaving New York around 8 a.m. and arriving in San Francisco at sunset.

    Chuck came to pick me up, and we spent two days together, because the *Laura Mærsk* had not yet arrived after traversing the Panama Canal. I was astonished how fast the plane had flown across the entire United States and that I beat the ship to San Francisco.

    I boarded the *Laura Mærsk* on April 11. To top off my delight, I was given back the pilot's cabin. My certificate of service as second waiter was signed by Captain Obel. It is shown on the next page, followed by three photos giving a glimpse of the ship's interior: the captain's dayroom, the passenger lounge with the Mærsk star woven into the carpet, and a typical passenger cabin sleeping three people.

Certificate of Service (Mønstringsbevis) for Eddie Lumsdaine, U.S.A., born Hong Kong 7/3-37, signed on 11/4-53 on the motor ship Laura Mærsk (LAURA MAERSK) of Copenhagen (København). Capacity: Waiter, 2' Tjener. Master: Sv. Aa. Obel. Port of destination: Østen t.v. – Far East and further. Port: New York, den 11 April 1953. Authority's signature: E. V. Ahlsen, Overstyrmand. Served as Waiter, 2 Tjener from 11/4-53 until 18/12-53. Master's signature: E. V. Ahlsen, Overstyrmand. Characteristics of voyage: Far East and U.S.A. Seaman discharged 18/12-1953. Port: San Francisco, den 18/12 1953.

Voyage to "New Gold Mountain"

Lounge

Captain's Dayroom

Cabin

9

Getting off at "Old Gold Mountain"

As the second waiter I had to greet all the passengers along with my colleague, the first waiter. My job was to clean the passenger cabins and captain's quarters, as well as help the first waiter set the tables, serve meals, and make sure the dining room and lounge were spic and span. I still remember carefully polishing the water spots off the glasses before placing the rolled-up crisp linen napkins at each place setting in the nicely furnished room (see photo below). The passengers dined with the captain, first mate, and chief engineer. Sometimes the chief steward was invited to join them—though normally, he dined with the officers. The first waiter provided extra comforts such as deck chairs or coffee and snacks.

Getting off at "Old Gold Mountain"

Early on Easter Sunday, April 12, 1953, we set sail for Manila, a twenty-day trip. After the passengers and officers had been served, we had a party that evening for all who were working under the chief steward—the boys, the cook, the baker, the first waiter, and a few others (including the wife of the chief steward who was accompanying him on this voyage). In the photo below, the first waiter is at the left edge, Kierkegaard at the right edge. This is my only picture that shows me wearing the white waiter's jacket.

My first passengers were quite a mixed group: a couple from Georgia, a handsome divorcee, an elderly widow, a wealthy young woman who had boarded the ship in Panama for an extended cruise, a retired railroad engineer with his wife, and a snake handler on his way to the Philippines to buy exotic reptiles. His arms showed many bites that he often displayed to the crew or passengers. He told me not to bother cleaning his room—he would leave the laundry in the hallway outside his door.

During designated hours, it was customary for me to knock on the passenger cabin doors. If there was no answer, or if invited, I would walk in to clean the room. About ten days into the trip to Manila, I inadvertently opened the snake handler's cabin door since I had received no answer to my knock. I did not find a snake pit but a startled snake handler in bed with the young divorcee. I quickly excused myself and later apologized profusely. Neither of them seemed embarrassed—apparently the snake handler was charming more than just snakes. This incident taught me to be more careful, and I did not make that mistake again.

The next day, the new cabin boy who was covered with tattoos knocked on my door. Holding up a deck of cards, he said, *"Hans, lader spiller poker, okay?"* It was easy to see he was eager to get into a game of poker. Since it was Sunday and my day off, I didn't need to think about this offer long. I sauntered over to the boys' cabin, and Kierkegaard, Tattoo-boy, the baker's helper, and I got into a poker game. The first day Tattoo-boy broke even, and the rest of us did not lose much to each other.

The games got more frequent the following week—almost every other night after work. Tattoo-boy started to win most of the time. Being a card shark myself, I began to keep a very close watch when he dealt the cards. When I saw him cheat, I immediately stood up and said to him, "I quit because I saw you deal a card from the bottom of the deck." Tattoo-boy became enraged, and as I walked from the cabin door into the hallway, he grabbed me by the collar and quickly punched me in the stomach and then my face.

I started to bleed heavily from my nose. The fourth engineer heard the noise in the hallway and came out to stop the fight. After this incident, I tried to avoid going to that part of the ship. It really made me wonder why, being in his mid-twenties, Tattoo-boy was still eking out a living as a

Getting off at "Old Gold Mountain"

cabin boy. In any case, my gambling days on board the ship were over quickly.

From Manila we went to Keelung and then to Takao, now known as Kaohsiung. It is a large port on the south end of Taiwan (the former Formosa). Then we continued straight to Hong Kong. We arrived in midmorning and were told to be back on board by 9 p.m. if we went ashore, because the ship would set sail at 10 p.m. I rushed to the Gaans but did not find them at home. I went to see Father Des who was delighted to see me. He asked me to bring a small box of baby clothes—booties, little shirts, pants and pajamas—to a family in New York. I gladly accepted the simple request, never dreaming how costly this would turn out to be.

From Hong Kong we first made the usual loop around the Far East to Bangkok and Saigon (now Ho Chi Minh City in Vietnam), followed by several ports in the Philippines before returning to Hong Kong. Next we started on another transpacific voyage to New York pretty much on the same itinerary as on my first journey, except that we went from Japan directly to San Francisco, skipping Vancouver. Also, this time, we did not have any storms nor boxing matches.

The *Laura Mærsk* arrived in New York on July 31. The customs officer who came into my cabin was filled with anger. He looked at me with eyes full of hate and practically tore up my cabin. He discovered a deep hole about one foot in diameter and several feet deep hidden behind the sofa cushions. He seemed convinced he would find something there. At the height of the Korean War he may have felt justified in his hate of anyone Chinese. Never mind that I proudly flashed an American passport.

Fortunately, the hole was empty. I still get the shivers

thinking of what would have happened if he had found something illegal left by a previous occupant of the room. I am certain I would have been sent to jail, and my entire life would have been ruined—the explanations of a Chinese boy would not have been believed.

The customs officer was furious that he could not discover anything among my belongings beyond the small box of baby clothing Father Des had given me to bring to New York. Almost gleefully he shoved a slip into my hand, explaining I had failed to declare this box and would be fined. The slip ordered me to appear in the downtown Customs Office on Monday, August 3. To ensure my appearance, he took my passport with him. The other boys had several undeclared items bought on the voyage, but they were ignored.

For three days, I was very anxious about not having my passport; I felt somehow I was in peril. When I went to the Customs Office at the appointed time, I was surprised to find Captain Obel there. He told me, "I think it is rather unlikely that you will get a fine."

When a clerk handed me a ticket, Captain Obel reached for it. When he read that Customs had not only confiscated the box but also fined me $10.05, he raised his voice to ask the customs official, "Do you know how much this boy makes in a week?" After a pause, he then answered his own question, "Ten dollars." Then, under his breath, he murmured, "This is ridiculous."

The customs clerk did not react, but just stamped the seizure notification (shown on the next page) after I paid the fine. He then passed it to me across the counter, together with my passport. As I took the ticket, the captain muttered quietly in Danish, "*Svindlere.*"

Getting off at "Old Gold Mountain"

Customs Form 5113 TREASURY DEPARTMENT 24.20, 24.21, 24.22, 24.22, C. M., 1948. July 1938	NOTICE AND ACCOUNT OF FINES, PENALTIES, AND FORFEITURES, AND RECEIPT

UNITED STATES CUSTOMS SERVICE

N? 380594

0944   District No. 10 , Port of N.Y. , Aug. 3, 1953. , 19

To   Master | Seizure or Case No. 59227

SS Laura Maersk , 19

Pay to the Cashier of Customs the sum of ******Ten****** 05/100 dollars

($ 10.05) on account of penalty imposed on Above
(Name of person, vessel, etc.)

for Failure to manifest & Mitigated Forf.
(Nature of offense)

in violation of 584 T.A. 1930
(Section) (Act or regulation)

Penalty by Department letter No. of , 19
(Mitigated, fine equal to duty, etc.)

MERCHANDISE	VALUE	RATE	DUTY
Paid by Edward Lumsdaive	PAID $	Master	6.00
	AUG 13 1953	Forf.	4.05
	CASHIER OF CUSTOMS NEW YORK 4, N.Y. $12		
		Clerk.	
		(Title)	

INSTRUCTIONS.—To be prepared IN TRIPLICATE; original to be forwarded to party from whom the account is due; duplicate retained or delivered to cashier as collection account—when paid, to be so stamped, and recorded as collection voucher; and triplicate retained as office record where prepared. When official receipt is requested by payor, or remittance does not identify the account for which payment is made, the ORIGINAL OF THIS NOTICE MUST ACCOMPANY THE REMITTANCE FOR THAT PURPOSE.

I was very relieved the case was over. I had my passport back, and the captain was not angry with me for having been summoned (I presume) to come all the way downtown to the Customs Office. As a result, my respect for Captain Obel increased by several degrees. But to this day, half a century later, I still have trouble forgiving that officer. On the other hand, the incident taught me an important lesson—to be fair-minded with people no matter who they are. Unfortunate events like these made me more sensitive to the occurrence of discrimination in whatever guise it appears. Not surprising, I have kept the seizure notice as a reminder all these years.

This time, we left New York after eleven days and sailed to Boston, Philadelphia, and Baltimore, then back to New York for another week's stay. I went ashore and bought an accordion and a harmonica. I could play the harmonica well but hoped to learn how to play the accordion in my free time at sea. After a couple of sessions, the captain ordered me to do my practicing astern!

The *Laura Mærsk* set sail for San Francisco by way of the Panama Canal and Los Angeles, crossing under the Golden Gate Bridge on September 16, 1953. By this time I was rather tired of being scolded by the new chief steward whom I could not please no matter how hard I worked. He could not report me to the captain since none of the passengers ever complained about me. In fact, the first waiter received praises for my courteous behavior. When the passengers left, they usually tipped quite well: $50 was typical for the two of us.

When I saw my brother Chuck briefly in San Francisco, I told him, "This is my last voyage on the *Laura Mærsk*—I'm planning to leave the ship the next time it docks here."

From San Francisco, the ship sailed to Manila, Cebu, San Fernando, Keelung, and then on to Hong Kong, arriving at 4 p.m. on October 17. Since we were due to sail out eight hours later, I did not dare go ashore—I didn't want to risk not getting back in time. To tell the truth, the main reason was to avoid seeing Father Des and having to confess that the small box of baby clothes he had entrusted to me had been confiscated.

As we were leaving Victoria Harbor after midnight, a motorized junk approached and two drunken seamen were flashing lights, yelling, and signaling to get on board. The captain halted the *Laura Mærsk*, and a net was lowered to haul the two truants up, one at a time. This behavior was not

Getting off at "Old Gold Mountain"

unusual and was rarely reprimanded—the long tedious voyages were taking a toll on some of the seamen. By now, I could empathize with such feelings.

After sailing to various ports in the Far East, we returned to Hong Kong on November 17. We arrived around 10 a.m. and stayed until 5 p.m. the next day. Because those were weekdays, I had to work. However, since I did want to go ashore this time, I negotiated with the first waiter that I would cover for him the second day if he would let me have the first evening off.

I went directly to the Gaan family. Mr. Gaan was away on business, but the two daughters and their mother welcomed me. The girls were once again very glad to see me and asked many questions about my adventures. Little did they know that the trips were becoming routine and boring. After dinner I quickly returned to the ship.

The trip from Hong Kong to San Francisco with stops at several ports—Keelung, Kobe, Nagoya, Yokohama, Shimizu, and then Vancouver—was uneventful except for a minor storm in the Pacific. One of the passengers returning from a two-month cruise to the Far East was an elderly widow from Baltimore. In talking with me she found out I was planning to leave the ship. She said I could live with her and help her take care of her big house and garden, and she even offered to pay for college later. I had no reason to turn down her kind offer—but it just didn't feel right and brought back memories of the incident with the sailor in Shanghai.

We docked in San Francisco on a foggy morning on December 17, 1953. I worked that entire day and then informed the chief mate I would collect my things and sign off the *Laura Mærsk* the next day. Since childhood I had known of San Francisco as the "Old Gold Mountain." In my mind I was now ready and determined to explore and claim the promises of the "Golden Gate."

Below is an excerpt of the Captain's Log, showing the last segments of my time aboard the *Laura Mærsk*. I have marked my final port with an arrow.

My brother was coming to pick me up—in his own car! We had stayed in touch through letters, and Chuck had tried to explain to me some of the basic differences between living in Shanghai and living in America. People in the United States were living without fear of arbitrarily being arrested, convicted, and even executed—it was a country ruled by law. It really was a land of unlimited opportunities. I was told anyone willing to work hard would be able to make it.

Getting off at "Old Gold Mountain"

Now that I was no longer an occasional visitor in a US port on shore leave but would actually settle down in this country, I couldn't wait to begin this new chapter in my life. After a journey of nearly eighteen months from when I left Shanghai, the desire of my heart was finally within my reach—claiming my birthright as an American, to *be* a real American. I was to find that the path to reach my dream was far different from what I had imagined.

10

Encounters in San Francisco

I left the *Laura Mærsk* in San Francisco on December 18, 1953. Although I had been the youngest second waiter in the A.P. Møller Shipping Company starting at age fifteen—and perhaps could have become first waiter and then chief steward someday—I felt this was not the path I wanted to take. Looking at the opportunities at sea, I realized I could never become a captain on a Danish ship. If I had the right education, I might become captain of an American ship. But my main desire at this time was to become a fighter pilot.

The decision to leave was not hard, although I had mixed feelings. The new chief steward was a crotchety old salt, with a mean streak, and impossible to please. But I had become good friends with the cook—we communicated mostly by sign language and broken Danish—and to some extent with the baker. Kierkegaard was leaving me alone, so things were peaceful. Also, the job as second waiter was fun—I met lots of interesting people, and the money (including tips from the passengers) was good.

Yet, the daily humdrum had chipped away at the original excitement of my job. Even the voyages touching on the same ports had become routine. I was ready for something new, even though I hadn't the foggiest idea of what I was looking for. In retrospect, I was utterly incapable of imagining the crucial turning point in my life I was to reach in just ten short months.

In the process of saying goodbye to everyone, I noticed

the chief steward was very angry. I had known for some time he had wanted me off the ship so he could promote one of the other boys to waiter. Thus I could not understand why he started to curse me as I signed out in the chief mate's cabin and withdrew all the funds from my ship's account. The chief mate had to sternly order him to shut his mouth and leave the cabin.

Saying farewell to the cook was more emotional. He gave me a big hug, and I asked him, "What's the problem with the chief steward?"

From his gestures and a few Danish words I got the idea that the chief steward was very, very jealous that I, a Chinaman, could go and live in America and he could not. In farewell, he said, "*Scribe,* Hans" while vigorously pointing to himself—he wanted me to write to him.

When I went into the cabin to say goodbye to Kierkegaard, he jumped off the top bunk, shook my hand, and then gently put his other hand on top of my head. For the first time I saw kindness in his deep blue eyes. He said in English, "Good journey, Hans." This was the only time he called me Hans. It seemed like a blessing for a good future. I was so touched I felt remorse—not too long ago I had wanted to kill him, and I had harbored hate for him during the entire time I was on the ship.

Both my father and brother were still in "Old Gold Mountain." My father lived in a tiny one-room apartment, subsisting as a janitor. Chuck was sharing a one-bedroom apartment with a friend. He invited me to live with them until I could find a job and move out on my own. He bought a camping bed, and I slept in the hallway. I gave Chuck most of my money to send to the family in Shanghai. He suggested I start looking for a job after Christmas, but I was very anxious and didn't want to wait even a day.

Chuck lived on Clay Street, and it was a good walk from there to Chinatown where I thought I might get a job as a waiter. I was very self-conscious about my Chinese features. But I hoped people would accept me as an American, even though I did not look white (which in those days seemed to be expected if one were an American). But as I walked around and listened to the Chinese chatter, it made me feel I was still in China. This was not what I had expected—I was seeking to fit in where I could be a real American. Thus I decided to look elsewhere for a job, especially since my English was much improved.

The next day, as I walked down Clay Street into Van Ness Avenue, I saw a "Help Wanted" sign for a soda jerk in the window of a small restaurant. I went in and ordered coffee with a sweet roll. I began talking with the cook and quickly found out that he was also the owner.

"I'd like to apply for the advertised job."

Rather gruffly, the owner replied, "You're too young."

"But I have lots of experience. I worked as a waiter for about a year on board a Danish ship."

"Sorry, I really have someone else in mind already."

That was my first encounter with job discrimination in America, although I now understand that this was during the Korean War, and a Chinese-looking man would not be welcome serving behind the counter.

A distinguished-looking man with graying hair sitting next to me at the counter overheard my conversation with the cook and began taking an interest in me. He spoke so kindly I opened up and told him about the recent events in my life. I explained, "I have to find a job and move out of my brother's apartment."

"I think I have a solution to your problem. I have a place nearby with two bedrooms. Why don't you move in with me—you can pay me when you start earning some money."

I was speechless and must have had a puzzled look on my face. Thus he quickly continued by introducing himself, "My name is Horace Filer. I work for an insurance company as a manager. I can also help you find a job."

Because many people had been kind to me since I left Shanghai without expecting anything in return, I felt I had stumbled onto another generous soul. Horace pulled out a small piece of paper and jotted down something before handing it to me. "Here is my phone number. Do call me as soon as you're ready to move in."

When I told my brother the exciting news, he and his friend just looked at each other. Chuck finally broke the silence, "See if Horace can come for dinner on Christmas Eve."

Horace was able to join us at Chuck's place as planned. My father was there as well but said little. My brother began probing the background of our guest with many personal (and I thought hostile) questions. Apparently, Horace graduated from Princeton with a B.S. and M.S. in mathematics and had been the principal of a high school in New Jersey. This did not impress me since I had no idea what graduating from a prestigious university and what those degrees meant.

Chuck then asked belligerently, "Why would you leave a job as principal to become an insurance agent?"

Horace corrected him by pointing out, "I'm a manager in an insurance company. I wanted to move west after spending all my life on the East Coast. I'm an only child, and my widowed mother still lives out East."

Chuck then asked, "What kind of a job are you going to find for my brother?"

Horace replied, "I don't know, but I will help him look through ads in the Sunday paper."

All during this interrogation, I desperately tried to steer the conversation in other directions, such as Christmas topics. I didn't care about Horace's background—all I cared about was that this man had room for me and that he appeared to be kind and generous. I was hoping my brother wouldn't insult him to where he would walk out. Later, as Horace was leaving, he gave me his address, and I was relieved to hear him say, "I'm usually home after 6 p.m. on weekdays and all day on weekends, but please call first before you come."

After Horace's departure, I asked my father and Chuck, "Well, what do you think about my moving in with Horace—since you have already lived in San Francisco for over two years?"

My father responded mildly, "Horace appears to be a nice man."

Chuck was more hesitant. "I want you to take me along when you're ready to go to Horace's place."

I was quite eager, and thus a few days after Christmas 1953, I moved in with Horace and learned some things I did not expect.

As soon as we arrived, Horace took me to my room. It was rather empty except for a table and chair. I was puzzled and asked, "Where do you want me to sleep?"

"Here," he laughed, opening up a set of doors and pulling down a bed. He showed us around, gave me a set of keys and then said, "Make yourself at home. I'm going to be away for a week."

I spent that time bumming around San Francisco and had a great New Year's Eve celebration at Chuck's place. By then, Chuck's early misgivings had abated, and he accepted my good fortune.

As I walked out of the apartment early in the morning two days later, I noticed a boy about my age with bags full of newspapers hanging from his shoulders, front and back. This sparked my curiosity and I approached him to start a conversation.

"Do you live around here?" I asked.

"I live in the Mission District, and my aunt brings me to this paper route before she goes to work nearby, man. But on weekends I have to take a bus here," he replied with a heavy accent.

Thus I inquired, "Where are you from?"

"My name is Hector Gutierrez and I'm from El Salvador," he revealed. "My divorced parents still live there."

I also found out he was one year older than I. Pointing to a place across the street, I asked, "Will you join me for a cup of coffee as soon as you are finished with your route?"

When in the coffee shop, Hector asked me all sorts of questions about myself, and in return I asked many questions about him. I felt a real kinship with him when he said, "I got kicked out of Galileo High School for bad conduct and now I have to attend Continuation High."

I confided, "I was kicked out of St. Joan of Arc in Shanghai and have not yet started back in school."

Then he said, "My brother and I live with my aunt Marianna. My father pays her for my keep—I'm just working to have pocket money."

This prompted me to ask, "How could I become a newspaper boy?"

Hector grinned and explained the paper delivery: "I buy

the papers from the *San Francisco Chronicle* at $1.50 per paper per month and collect $2.00 per paper per month from my customers."

"This sounds like something I could do well."

He suggested, "Why don't we meet with my boss, the route manager, when he drops off the papers for my route tomorrow morning?" Then he gave me precise directions to the location.

The paper delivery was usually promptly at 6 a.m., but this Sunday, it was twenty minutes late. As the papers were dropped off, Hector and I waved to attract attention and quickly approached the route boss to talk to him. The man revealed, "A route is opening closer to where you live, Hector. If you would take that route, Edward can take your present assignment."

Hector agreed to switch. The route manager then requested, "Please call the next day to get it all set up. I don't have time to do this right now."

I spent most of the day with Hector, accompanying him on his paper route and later going over to his house to have a simple but delectable dinner of tortillas, refried beans, a bit of meat, and salad. When I asked about his brother, Hector said matter-of-factly, "He is away and won't be around for at least a year." It didn't take long to find to my amazement that Hector knew almost all the bus routes in San Francisco.

The best way to describe Hector today is to say that in his mannerisms he closely resembled "the Fonz" of *Happy Days*. When years later I saw that television serial, it was uncanny how much Fonzie reminded me of Hector. Because Hector was Latino, he did not look like the Caucasian Henry

Winkler, the actor who portrayed "the Fonz," but he was so very cool, exactly like Fonzie.

By mid-January my brother Chuck grew concerned because I was not enrolled in school. One day he drove me over to Galileo High, which was near Fisherman's Wharf. The school counselor gave me a battery of tests and asked Chuck to bring me back in a couple of days.

When we returned, I discovered I had done so poorly I could not be admitted even to the ninth grade, although I was already sixteen. The counselor mentioned that my IQ was below normal. Chuck explained, "Edward is multilingual and speaks Danish quite well, but he has trouble reading English since it is not his native tongue."

The counselor then suggested to Chuck, "The best place for him would be in Continuation High until the end of the school year—with his low scores he would never be able to catch up with a regular curriculum."

My brother was very disappointed at this outcome, but I was happy because I knew Hector was at that school.

I found out there was more than one Continuation High in the City of San Francisco. The one I was assigned to was full of misfits, thugs, dropouts and those just released from juvenile detention. There were also a few immigrants who couldn't speak or write English well and could not get into a regular high school (I guess like me). I was told I was reading at a fifth grade level—I was surprised it was even that good. On the other hand I found I had no trouble at all keeping up with high school math.

My day started with the ring of the alarm clock at 5:30 a.m. After delivering *The Chronicle*, I walked over to Chuck's place and he would give me a ride to school. Then to get home in late afternoon, I took a bus.

I delivered about 150 papers per day. My route consisted entirely of apartment buildings on hilly streets. I often had to climb several flights of stairs—many buildings had no elevators. On Sundays it took twice as long because I could only carry half as many of the heavy editions at a time in the front and back pouches.

At the end of January, I went around to collect for the month's payment. I paid the route boss for the whole month and then gave Hector his share of the money for the time he had delivered the papers. I ate many meals with Hector and gave Marianna some money for my food. I also gave money to Horace, which he appreciated.

With the end of February coming up, I did not want to go around all the apartments again to collect for the month. The previous month, it had been difficult to find some of the people at home; others told me to come back because they didn't have the money right then, and a couple had even moved away without telling me and paying me. Thus, I placed a bunch of self-addressed envelopes without stamps in my customers' mailboxes, with a note to please mail in their two dollars. I had about a fifty percent response.

In March, I placed a 3-cent stamp on the self-addressed envelopes and received nearly an eighty-five percent response, although this cost me five bucks. But it was worth the investment because it saved lots of time. I enjoyed being an entrepreneur and coming up with "better ways of doing things." Moreover, I saved many extra steps by generously tipping the doormen in the taller apartment buildings for taking the papers up to the individual tenants. This boost in efficiency allowed me to add more streets to my paper route, thus increasing my profit.

For more income, I began to look for after-school work and landed a job as an usher in a movie theatre close by. This was only three evenings a week but suited me fine.

Horace and I got along well. We ate some meals together, and he was an excellent cook. I enjoyed our easy conversations. For example, I could chime in and criticize the US President—not that I had any knowledge or strong opinion, but just because I could. Under the Communists in China especially, we were not even allowed to whisper anything against the government without risking a jail sentence.

He asked me to muffle the alarm clock because he wanted to get up at 7 a.m., not at 5:30 a.m. since he had a long day. I wedged my alarm clock into a pillow, and that did the trick. On weekends, Horace often helped me with my English homework.

I found it odd that Horace had never married and didn't even have a girlfriend. He occasionally had people over for dinner—a male colleague or a female coworker and spouse. Once in a while, he would spend an evening with friends but did not leave a phone number. I did not ask questions—I thought his social life was none of my business. But by the end of April, I began to see a different side to Horace.

One evening, he came home with a colleague from work who was Chinese. The conversation turned to China during World War II. Horace pointed out, "Millions of additional Chinese would have died if it hadn't been for the atom bomb."

The topic then moved on to intelligence. The visitor began by saying, "With so many people in China, the number of intelligent Chinese there is bound to exceed the number of intelligent Americans in the US. Besides, most of the stuff in the West was invented in China and 'stolen' by the West."

The Chinese colleague began to explain about the culture and the early inventions made in China. He also mentioned, "The Western US would not be anywhere near as well off, had it not been for the Chinese building the entire railroad system from the Pacific coast to the Midwest."

I listened with rapt attention and gained a new respect for being part Chinese.

Horace on the other hand was furious. He raised his voice and yelled, "The Americans fed the Chinese after the war, yet now they are so ungrateful and fight the Americans in Korea." The more he spoke, the angrier he got.

I became frightened, and the Chinese colleague got up and left abruptly. Horace started to laugh as if the whole thing had been a joke. That scared me even more—I could not understand how someone could exhibit such opposite attitudes and change moods so quickly.

Also in April, Horace asked if I would go to a movie with him. In the middle of the show, he put his right hand on my left thigh and began to rub. I thought he was just being friendly. It made me uncomfortable, but I ignored it. When the show ended, Horace acted as if nothing unusual had happened. But several days later, while I was taking a bath, he came in and offered to wash me. I politely declined, saying I could do it myself. He insisted, and then he scrubbed me in inappropriate ways and places.

The next day I told Hector all about it. Hector responded, "Hey, man, he is queer." Then Hector, using street talk that I cannot repeat here, very graphically explained what "queers" do and what I could expect. He opened a dresser drawer where he kept half a dozen switchblades.

Hector picked one, extended it to me, and said, "Here, take this one—it has a four-inch blade. Next time he messes with you, man, you tell him you don't travel that road. If he tries to rape you, you cut off his balls." He explained, "You would never have to do time because you are underage."

I was skeptical because I was Chinese; I did not think I could get a fair trial since public feelings ran high against the Chinese because of the Korean War. But Hector insisted I keep the switchblade.

A week later in school, the math teacher needed to cut something during a demo and asked if anyone had a pocketknife. I walked to the front and proudly handed over my switchblade. The teacher asked me, "Do you know it is illegal to carry this type of knife?"

I don't know what possessed me to say yes.

At the end of his lesson, the teacher handed the knife back to me without a word.

After class Hector walked with me and commented, "Hey, Eduardo—that took some guts. Word is going to get around, and nobody in this school is going to mess with you, man. You don't need my protection anymore." He laughed. From then on I left the switchblade at the apartment.

Things were back to normal with Horace. We even went to a movie in early May without incident. However, a few days later, he came home drunk. He started to kiss me and fondle me with his hands where he had no business. I ran to pick up my knife, popped out the switchblade, and warned him, "Don't you ever touch me like that again!" He sobered up quickly.

I immediately took a bus to Hector's apartment and told him what had happened. Hector came up with a plan: "When Horace goes to work, I will go with you to get your stuff. You can share my room." When Hector told his aunt about this arrangement, she chuckled and said, *"Está aquí todo el tiempo como quiera."*

Hector translated, "He's here all the time anyway."

Having lived with Horace would have unforeseen and long-lasting consequences in my future career and life—something that in today's changed culture could not even be conceived.

It was great living with Hector. I gladly helped him with his newspaper route when I was finished with mine—he really hated to get up early. Hector taught me Spanish and translated everything his aunt said when I didn't understand. The only thing that caused friendly arguments between us was our different taste in music. We resolved this by agreeing to have jazz hours for him and semi-classical hours for me.

Hector had several girlfriends and introduced me to one of them, named Iliana, with whom I attended a movie now and then. One day I bought two expensive tickets to a concert by the San Francisco Philharmonic Orchestra. The music was glorious, but Iliana fell asleep before the intermission. I never asked her out again.

In some ways I was world-wise because of the years of living in the streets of Shanghai and working on the *Laura Mærsk*. However, I saw Hector as having street smarts the American way. In general, I was still quite shy and self-conscious about being Chinese and different—not a real American. I was envious of Hector who also was not an American but able to mingle, get chicks, and gain respect from real Americans. I discovered a few weeks later how wrong I was.

Hector had a blue 1950 souped-up Ford. His father had

bought him the car when he turned seventeen, and he fixed it up to look cool. One Saturday when we drove on the Bayshore Freeway, a patrol car stopped us. A cop came over and scrutinized Hector.

Even before looking at Hector's driver's license, he barked, "You a wetback?"

"I am from Central America, not Mexico," growled Hector in reply.

The cop took offense and bellowed, "Okay, wetback, get the hell out of the car." Next, he demanded I get out as well.

Then the officer searched the car. He ordered Hector to raise his arms and patted him down. Finally, he allowed us to get back in the car, and he gruffly handed Hector a ticket for speeding.

As we pulled back into traffic, I saw Hector blow up—for the first time. He swore in Spanish, and then he said, "This is the kind of s--- that makes me hate this f--- country. I don't belong here." I was stunned because I had thought he fit in so well whereas I was the misfit who desperately wanted to be like him.

By the end of summer I was admitted to Galileo High. When school started, I found it offered no real challenge. I often walked to Fisherman's Wharf from school to eat my sack lunch. I was restless and felt I wanted to move on—to excitement and adventure just beyond the horizon. Also, I had begun to realize that with my skimpy educational background and my Chinese features, I had few if any options for finding a good job.

One day, Hector and I hatched out a plan for our future. We agreed that the morning following my seventeenth birthday we would meet at the recruiting station after our paper jobs and sign up for the US Navy—Hector preferred the Navy to being drafted into the Army. Thus on the appointed day, I went to the Naval Recruiting Station off Market Street with my father. Because of my age, I needed parental permission.

We waited for hours for Hector, but he did not show. I became more and more agitated. I realized I was choosing the Navy only because of Hector. I really preferred the Air Force because I wanted to be a pilot. I asked my father, "Would you mind if we went across the street to the Air Force recruiters, so I can sign up with them?" Just this impulsively, I found myself committed to the US Air Force for four years of drastic change and a new path for education.

The sergeant asked, "When can you be ready to report for basic training at Parks Air Force Base in Pleasanton?"

"I need about two weeks to take care of some personal matters."

This was not strictly true, because all I really wanted was to take a few days off to loaf around. Little did I know this was the last time the Air Force asked me what I wanted—from then on I would always be told what to do.

About a year after I entered the Air Force, my brother Chuck was drafted into the Army. A year after that, Hector was drafted and sent to Korea.

Looking back at the first seventeen years of my life, my father's signature for me to join the US Air Force was his last act that directly influenced the direction of my life. It turned out to be an important step in my goal of becoming a true American.

11

Military Training

On 18 October 1954, I began basic training in the United States Air Force at Parks Air Force Base. We—a group of fifteen new recruits—were taken by bus from downtown San Francisco to Pleasanton. When I signed up, I was given a list of items we were allowed to take to basic training. It was easy to merely pack a small bag since I didn't have many possessions.

The sergeant who accompanied us to the base was a mild-mannered person. As soon as we arrived, we were met by the technical instructor (or T.I.), and all hell broke loose. From my fourteen months on the Danish ship I was used to being yelled at. But now I was introduced to a new phase of being a "low life." I had to do everything as I was told, and it had to be done the Air Force way. The more exactly orders were followed, the better. Since I had a mind for doing things my way, this was a difficult adjustment.

Almost immediately, the T.I. yelled at us, "Stand shoulder to shoulder!" After introducing himself, he told us to address him as "Sir" every time we opened our mouths. He had only two stripes (showing his rank was airman second class), but for us he might as well have been a general.

The T.I. walked over to the biggest recruit who had a large, bulging bag and barked, "Dump out all your belongings!" He stood there for a moment, scrutinizing the pile and shaking his head.

Then the T.I. pushed his nose almost up to the guy's

cheek and squeaked, "Why in the world did you bring such stupid items with you to basic training? Do you sleep with a teddy bear?"

"No," said the recruit. This brought a barrage of insults—he had omitted to add, "Sir."

The T.I. screamed, "I want you to say, 'No, Sir' five times so the whole base can hear you!"

I didn't understand why he needed to humiliate this guy like that, but I suppose it was part of our training. On the other hand, our T.I. never used profanity or racial slurs.

Decades later, when I was Distinguished Visiting Professor at the US Air Force Academy, I jokingly told a cadet in one of my classes to "shut up." The cadets laughed it off as a jest. A colonel who was an observer in the class reprimanded me that *The Code* required instructors to be respectful when interacting with the cadets. How times have changed since I was in basic training.

The day after reporting to basic training, I received the prescribed haircut—total removal of hair down to mere stubble. A few days later, we were issued uniforms according to our weight, height, and body build. The most important measurements were hat and shoe size, and all headgear as well as boots and shoes were carefully fitted. Some of the others complained, but I thought these were the finest clothes I had in my entire life.

I was placed in a barracks (designated a dormitory) with other airmen in what was called a Flight. A number of Flights made up a Squadron, and a number of Squadrons made up a Wing.

We called each other by last names or by nicknames. The two I remember most were a rather stocky farm boy from

Military Training

the Bluegrass State we dubbed "Kentucky" and Merdinck who couldn't seem to do anything right. Kentucky became our barracks chief or supervisor. At age 26 he was older and more mature than most of us. Although we were all called "knuckleheads" by the T.I. at one time or another, Merdinck took special honors for being a knucklehead's knucklehead.

I learned that the toilets were called latrines, and KP or kitchen patrol meant peeling tons of potatoes and washing hundreds of pots and pans. I didn't mind doing KP, but some of my fellow airmen hated it. There were no filter cigarettes in those days, and we were taught to field strip our cigarette butts when smoking outdoors by removing and scattering the tobacco left in the butt, then rolling up the tiny remnant of paper, putting it into a pocket, and later disposing of it in a proper waste receptacle.

It continued to be hard for me to obey everything I was told every minute of the day. For example, I had to keep my footlocker tidy, my shoes and visor "spit and polished," and my bunk bed made in a particular way. Each weekday started with reveille at 5 a.m. and ended at 9 p.m. ("twenty-one hundred hours" in military terms). But Sunday was mostly a day of rest.

Some of my fellow airmen complained daily about the T.I., the living conditions, and the food. I, however, found the food to be very good. I especially liked a breakfast dish called S.O.S. that consisted of ground beef in a thick white sauce served on toast. Also, I drank gallons of fresh milk. The T.I. said he didn't like any of us. He often repeated, "My dog is smarter than you." He also was fond of growling, "By the time I get through with you, you will always remember me on Mother's Day." No one dared to laugh.

Then in groups of eight, we were brought into a room—

called the gas chamber—filled with tear gas. We wore our gas masks in and then were told to remove the masks and sing, "God Bless America." Merdinck got so sick he had to be taken out. The rest of us could put our masks back on but had to remain in the chamber for a while. If the masks were put on improperly, this would have been tough. We eventually emerged from the chamber coughing, but with nothing more serious than red, teary eyes. In addition, at the firing range we all had to learn to shoot a carbine—a light, semi-automatic rifle with a short barrel.

Basic training lasted ninety days. At graduation, our Flight with many others had to march for review by the base commander. The day before the review, the T.I. told me I had to carry the guidon—the squadron's flag—at the head of the

Flight. I was directed to snap my head and look at the review stand at his shout of "eyes right" and then lower the flag. I knew by then how to march in formation, but I didn't have a clue of what he was talking about. However, I didn't want to appear dumb—that would only make him yell at me—so I replied, "I understand, Sir."

Luckily I found someone who showed me exactly what to do. In the afternoon I practiced for hours. I was able to carry out the assignment without embarrassing myself or the T.I. After the parade the T.I. shook everyone's hand in congratulation, except Merdinck's; he had been told to report to sickbay on the day of graduation. By now, I admired my T.I. for his

Military Training

strength of character, discipline and integrity, and I had even started to like him.

With basic training completed, I felt a sense of accomplishment and satisfaction—I had not only survived but done well.

In January 1955, I was assigned for technical training to Keesler Air Force Base in Biloxi, Mississippi. I was placed in the Radio Intercept School, mainly because in a battery of tests I had the highest scores for radio operator, and possibly also because I spoke several languages, including Mandarin, Cantonese, and Shanghai dialect. All intercept operators were required to have a secret military clearance, which involved a thorough background check. This investigation initiated a sequence of events that would haunt me for many years to come.

On the base I roomed with three airmen—Otie Bottoms, Jim Newman, and Freddy Peeples who was black. Otie insisted that we call him by his first name. He dubbed me "Hong Kong" which I mildly resented since I wanted to blend in as an American. By calling me "Hong Kong" he was labeling me as a Chinese. But I did not correct him since he was not malicious nor using racial slurs—after all, I was born in Hong Kong and had lived there for a few months as a teenager, and thus the nickname could be construed (with a stretch) as based on truth.

In Mississippi, I came face-to-face with racial segregation. Before arriving there, I barely had an inkling of what this was all about. The Air Force was totally integrated by then, but outside Keesler Air Force Base this was another matter—another world. After three weeks on the base, I hitched a ride with one of the airmen on base who dropped me off in downtown Biloxi. As I walked around, I noticed separate drinking fountains, one with a sign "White" and another with a sign "Colored."

When I needed to use a public restroom, I found the same signs there as well. I had not been briefed by anyone about segregation and truly did not know which restroom to use. To be on the safe side, I walked into the "colored" restroom and startled a black man just walking out.

When I returned to the base I asked Newman, "Which restroom should I use?"

He laughed and said, "You can use either one."

This didn't sound reassuring — I suspected that he was joking and didn't really know the right answer. So I thought to myself that in the future I would only go to town as part of a group.

A week later, my roommates and I wanted to go into town together. We got on a bus and noticed the front of the bus was rather crowded, but the back of the bus was empty. Since it was an unusually warm day for February, the four of us moved to the back and plopped into the spacious seats.

After a few minutes the bus driver yelled, "You white boys, move to the front." We heard him but ignored him.

At the next stop he put on the parking brake and walked to the back. He threatened, "You white boys either move to the front or I'm gonna throw you off this here bus."

Newman looked at us and asked, "Shall we get off?"

To my relief we all made for the exit, and I didn't have to decide whether to move forward or stay with Peeples in the back.

Here is an experience I think is funny now, but not when it happened. I do not recall ever going into town again, but a group of us took a trip to Jacksonville, Florida. Peeples and I

Military Training

were the only two non-whites in the group. One airman told us that we were lucky to have dark skin because we could stay out in the sun for an extended period without getting sunburned. Peeples knew better, but I stayed out at the beach for hours believing the story. Needless to say, my back became severely sunburned. I went to sick-call for some treatment but continued to attend classes; I did not want to incur disciplinary action as a consequence of my credulity.

I found our training very interesting. The main emphasis was on learning the Morse code and how to type. We also learned how radios and antennas worked. To graduate from radio operator school, we had to achieve a certain typing speed—words per minute—with only a minimum number of errors. We also had to be able to send and receive Morse code at a prescribed number of words per minute. I was so proud to be able to send and receive faster than any of my classmates, and I had the highest score in the written tests. On the other hand, two guys in class could type faster than I could. The training lasted more than five months at forty hours a week. The graduation photo of our radio operator class is given on the next page.

Rumor had it that the person with the overall best score in the class could get his choice of overseas assignments. I requested France, England, or Spain because I really wanted to see Europe. When I received my orders, they indicated "APO 74 San Francisco," which I was sure was the post office box for Paris. I soon learned it was Clark Air Force Base in the Philippines. I was disappointed because I felt I had experienced enough of life in the Far East. However, this change in my plans turned out to be an unexpected blessing for my family.

In this June 1955 photo of my graduation class, I'm the third from the left in the top row.

President Harry S. Truman had issued an executive order in July 1948 to integrate the military. Change did not happen quickly, but within a generation, the US military became one of the country's most racially integrated institutions. The first combat test came during the Korean War and showed that integrated units worked well. To me, the contrast between the cooperative, comfortable, fully integrated Air Force Base and segregated Biloxi was a new experience and very startling.

12

Ups and Downs in the Philippines

After a few days of leave in mid-June 1955, I was flown to San Francisco to be shipped to the Philippines. I had hoped that being in the Air Force would mean we would be transported by airplane. Instead, I was literally shipped out on a Navy transport along with several hundred airmen, army men, and marines going to the Philippines for a tour of duty. The trip was rough, but I still had my sea legs and did not get seasick—unlike many of the other GI's.

On board ship, various groups were playing pinochle or poker for small wagers, and thus I played poker nearly every night. We used matchsticks as chits and settled the money later. It helped pass the time and I won moderate amounts.

Clark Air Force Base on southern Luzon near sea level was the home of the 13th Air Force, which included a squadron of F-86 Sabre jets. The Japanese Air Force had operated from this base just a few short years before (until 1945). I was assigned to the 14th Comm Squadron. The climate was hot and humid most of the year and unbearable in mid-summer. During the monsoon season from July through September, it rained buckets for days on end.

The base was next to Angeles City, which catered to the airmen from the base with hundreds of bars lining the main streets. Colorful jitneys (small, inexpensive buses) were everywhere. I was different from most of my colleagues in that I ventured beyond the usual hangouts of the airmen and made contact with local people, and I learned to speak some

Tagalog (pronounced "tug-ah-log"), the official language of the Philippines.

Like in China, the primary diet was rice, which I enjoyed. Sometimes it was mixed with sauce and meat. The rice was mostly eaten by rolling it up into a ball with fingers and popping it into the mouth while in a squatting position. I had no trouble eating with my fingers, but squatting for hours like the people who grew up here was impossible for me. Of course, in most homes I visited, knives and forks were used.

Although I was rather adventurous in trying many different local dishes, there was one I never tried—partially formed duck embryo called *balut*.

I asked a Filipino friend, "How can you eat *balut*?"

He replied, "It is a delicacy consisting of meat and soup—don't think of it as an egg. You Americans ..."

I was always proud when someone called me an American, and so I listened attentively, as he continued, "You eat insect spit, don't you?" I emphatically denied this.

"Well," he countered, "you just call it honey."

The regular radio operators handled most of the non-classified messages coming in and out of the base. The intercept operators handled the classified messages in rooms with a guarded entry. Filipino civilians manned many of the regular stations for both teletype and telegraph, as did intercept operators awaiting secret clearance. Weather reports for pilots came in by Morse code from around the world. Most of the stations used the *bug,* a mechanized Morse system that sent messages several times faster than the standard Morse code key.

I had expected to be assigned to the guarded rooms for

the intercept operators. Instead, I was assigned to work on the teletype. I was fascinated with the bug and thus I asked permission to work in one of the weather stations using it.

A few weeks later, I was given orders to remain in the non-classified area, and I was transferred without explanation out of a fifteen-man dormitory to a private room. This  special privilege was normally reserved for bachelor officers. I believed then and for a long time thereafter that I was separated from my peers because I still had close relatives in Communist China. Every so often I also thought the FBI had found out I had been less than upstanding when growing up in Shanghai and thus was not fit to get a secret clearance. I would not discover the truth until years later. The photo above shows me studying in my bright new room.

In the meantime, Chuck, my father, and Maria were working to get an exit visa for my mother and the remaining six children still in Shanghai. When the Communist government refused to grant the visas—we think mainly because the government desperately wanted to get hold of US currency—my mother asked one of my cousins traveling to Hong Kong to relay a message to my brother Chuck: "Stop sending money from the US." The monthly support payment was only $100—all that was allowed by US government regulation. We doubted that this was the reason for our family not getting the exit visa, but we did as she asked, although it made us feel horrible.

Within two months, my mother applied for welfare,

claiming she had no means of support because the family in the US had abandoned her and the children. This sounded plausible, because many Americans who had fathered children with Chinese wives simply abandoned them when they were released from Japanese internment. My school friend Alex Woodhouse's father was among them. I have always respected my father for his faithfulness to his family, no matter what the circumstances.

Of course, welfare in China consisted merely of allotments of rice and a very small stipend. Although the next few months of barely subsisting on the meager rations were very difficult, this drastic measure eventually caused the Communist government to grant the entire family exit visas to Hong Kong.

My mother and my younger siblings arrived in Hong Kong a few weeks after I was transferred to the Philippines. I immediately requested and was granted a one-week hardship leave and was given free passage on an Air Force plane flying to Hong Kong.

When I arrived in Hong Kong, I had no idea where my family was staying. On a hunch that my cousin Ho Siu Hwa might have some news, I hired a cab to take me to her apartment. She indeed knew they were staying with the "friends" that had found refuge with us when the Communists entered Shanghai. My family was not welcomed by Hung Tzer because she did not want to put up seven people.

My cousin divulged that James did get a permanent position at the Catholic School, but to please not let anyone in the family know about the crucial role I had played in his getting the job. Westerners have a hard time understanding this behavior called "saving face." James in time advanced to department head and taught there until his retirement.

Ups and Downs in the Philippines

Ho Siu Hwa then took me to my family. When my mother saw me, she burst out in tears. This was only the second time ever that I heard her cry outright. Usually, even when she was in severe pain, she would merely moan. She sobbed, "I don't have any money. We had to leave everything behind in Shanghai. The only thing I tried to bring, the small carved table, was confiscated at the border. Now I can't even rent an apartment."

I was glad I had saved up some money by then that I happened to carry with me. Thus I was able to tell her, "Mom, I can give you enough cash for a small apartment and groceries for a few months."

I promised, "I will apply for a monthly allotment for you as soon as I get back to Clark Air Force Base."

My cousin Ho Siu Hwa knew how I had been treated in Shanghai. She turned to my mother and said in Cantonese, "You treated him as the worst child and he turned out to be the best child."

My mother did not reply to Ho Siu Hwa, nor did she ever apologize, but for the rest of her life she made a special effort to cook my favorite dishes like steamed buns filled with barbecued pork whenever I visited her. Thus my being stationed in the Philippines turned out to be a long-term blessing for me, too. The photo on the preceding page shows my family in Hong Kong, with Robert, George, our mother and Philip in the back, and Milly, Albert and Dolly in the front.

By late 1955 I was working as a radio operator and flying regularly between Hong Kong and the Philippines on an Air Force C-47 (DC-3). I was a frequent visitor at the American Consulate, trying to get visas for the rest of the family to go to the US. Since I was in the military, the people at the Consulate were fairly accommodating and would tell me where in their pipeline the paperwork was being processed. However, at times I felt I came very close to being thrown out as a nuisance.

I learned the Gaans were no longer in Hong Kong. They had moved to Bangkok (and would later move to Los Angeles). Instead, I became friends with the Senna family who had two daughters, Betty and Anita. I had known them previously in Shanghai and always had a crush on Betty. Before long, we started to talk about marriage.

During those months, I did not do much else except work at my job, study, and jump at any opportunity to fly to Hong Kong. Since I expected to go to Officer Candidate School at the end of my tour of duty and then on to pilot training, I began learning how to fly a Piper Cub. Also, I took and passed courses in aeronautics and meteorology.

Then sometime in mid-1956 I received a "Dear John" letter from Betty—she had found someone else. I was crushed and did not know how to handle it. As a result of that breakup, I started my gambling again. With more than half of my salary going to the allotment supporting my mother and siblings in Hong Kong, I did not have much spare money to spend, but plenty of opportunities.

I met some Filipino acquaintances off base who were of Chinese descent. They got together often to play *mahjong*, which was still my favorite game. We would play at least twice a week, sometimes a whole night through. These were friendly games with low stakes, and as a rule I did not lose much. Still, my gambling losses made it impossible to continue the flying lessons.

One evening, one of the regular players invited me to a poker game in a place nearby. When I got there, five people were waiting already. Each one had to buy in for a specific sum and produce the cash on the table. We played draw poker for several hours, and by 2 a.m. I had taken in much of the money. I stacked up the bills and told the group, "I am finished," since I had to go to work early. One guy pulled out a .45 caliber pistol and told me, "Sit down! I will decide when we are finished!" By 5:30 a.m., when he called it quits, I had lost everything I had won and most of my own money.

Another time I and another airman were in a poker game where one of the players was wearing dark glasses indoors—he explained he had an eye problem. He seemed to guess when one of us was bluffing or had a lucky hand, and thus he was able to fold at the right time. Needless to say he was winning. I asked to be the dealer and also demanded a new deck of cards. This, however, did not change the outcome. When I had lost all my money, I left.

A few days later, I heard from one of the Filipino radio operators about traveling con men who found unsuspecting suckers like me. They used marked decks and through their special glasses could tell exactly which cards each player held. Very likely they operated in cahoots with the house.

When I flew to Hong Kong, I came across many women who wanted to date me. Also, my mother tried hard to get me interested in a nice Chinese girl I could marry. Even though she had married a Caucasian, she wanted her children to marry Chinese. But I did not listen to her.

Instead, my next girlfriend was another girl originally from Shanghai and half Caucasian—Nonie Britto. She was four years older than I and had one sibling, a younger sister about my age. Our relationship lasted only three months since she was insanely jealous. One day, Nonie's sister asked if I could take her shopping. When Nonie saw me walking downtown with her sister, she wrote me an angry letter, telling me she never wanted to see me again.

The photo on the left shows me and my colleague wearing parachutes—ready for a flight from Hong Kong back to the Philippines.

Then I was introduced to Esther—she was half Filipina and half Chinese. She was the daughter of one of the senior Filipino pilots from Quezon City. She was living and working in San Fernando, which was only a short jitney ride from Angeles City. We became quite serious and talked about marriage.

Esther's father had been a guerrilla during World War II. The Air Force had given me wilderness survival training, but that was nothing compared to his abilities. Naturally, I admired him greatly. Once, he and two other ex-guerrillas took me to one of the small islands to camp out for a few days. He hunted with his rifle, and we had plenty of meat to supplement the rice we had brought with us. The only thing that didn't taste good was the black "coffee" he made from charred rice.

One time when I was in the home of Esther's parents, her mother cooked a really great dinner. In the center was a small dish of what looked like meat in a dark sauce. I tried all the dishes including that one. The family members looked at each other and began to give each other the "evil smile." That's when I asked, "What is in this dish?"

"We'll tell you later."

They did. With more than a few chuckles, they said, "The mystery dish was bat meat."

"It was delicious," I responded. I really meant it.

They nodded, smiled at each other again, and then unanimously replied, "Oh, you're just being polite."

Since I frequently had to fly on assignments out of Clark Air Force Base to Hong Kong as well as Japan, I could not see Esther as often as I would have liked. When I returned from one of these trips unannounced, I found that another airman was living with her in her apartment. This was quite a shock to me, and I immediately broke off with her. These three unhappy love affairs during my Air Force years made it harder for me to form a trusting relationship with women in the future.

I had two close friends in my squadron: Hetland and Corson. Often, Hetland and I would go into Manila together since neither of us drank and Angeles City consisted only of bars. On one trip, we entered a restaurant to have dinner, and to my great surprise there was the second waiter from the *Laura Mærsk*, whom I had replaced when he left the ship in New York. With two other seamen, he was heavily into drinking beer.

He began by telling me, "I'm now the first waiter on the *Laura Mærsk*. She is docked at the port in Manila." Quite astonished he continued, *"Hans, hvorfor er du her* (Hans, why are you here)?"

I explained proudly, "I am in the United States Air Force now and stationed at Clark Air Force Base." Then I enquired, "How is it going with the chief steward?"

The first waiter somewhat gleefully shared, "The steward died at sea and the ship's crew *kastede ham oceanet* (threw him into the ocean)."

He had not liked that crotchety old man either. I must confess I was pleased to hear about the chief steward's fate.

Corson also broke up with his girlfriend. So he and I went in a jeep to Baguio, a favorite rest and recreation spot for GIs up in the mountains in the northern part of Luzon, with temperatures at a perfect twenty degrees Celsius, in contrast to the stifling heat at Clark Air Force Base.

The drive in the jeep was fun. I asked, "When did you learn how to drive?"

He explained, "I've handled vehicles on my family's farm since I was fourteen." He glanced at me and asked, "Do you want to drive?"

Surprise showed on his face when I answered, "I don't know how. Of all the families I knew when growing up in Shanghai, none had owned, driven, or even been near a car."

"Well, we have to fix this, don't we?" Then and there, Corson taught me how to drive the jeep, even though I didn't have a learner's permit. I learned quickly. In two months I was checked out and got a military driver's license.

Ups and Downs in the Philippines

Overseas assignments typically were for eighteen months. Thus by late 1956 my tour of duty in the Philippines was nearly complete. By then I had achieved respectable scores on the GED (educational equivalent to a high school diploma) and also passed the test for entry into Officer Candidate School.

One day I was called into the Office of Special Investigations (OSI). I was elated because I thought this was the final step before being sent to Officer Candidate School. At least five people were there, all in civilian clothes. Their questions seemed very strange, because they related to my friendship with other airmen, as well as people and places I visited while in Hong Kong and Japan, rather than to my Chinese relatives or my loyalty to the Air Force and the US.

After the meeting with the OSI I expected to receive orders for reassignment to stateside duty. Instead, I was given an indefinite extension of my stay in the Philippines. I was surprised but not unhappy since this made it possible to stay closer to my mother and siblings in Hong Kong. However, I did not understand the extension, and the Air Force never gave me an explanation.

Hetland and Corson had been called into the OSI, and they suddenly distanced themselves from me. Hetland stopped having regular coffee breaks with me. Corson, who was matter of fact about most things, now acted very aloof. I was perplexed by their withdrawal and began to miss our previous, warm camaraderie.

Three months later, a new commanding officer took over our squadron. A few days after his arrival, he called me into his office and told me these cryptic words, "I am sending you back to the States; their investigation of you can continue there if they wish." Although I became more and more baffled, I still thought this was because I had relatives living in Communist China.

Only years later I finally discovered the reason was my having shared an apartment with Horace, a gay man. Strangely, I was never asked outright about our relationship—it was all innuendo. Ironically, having lived in Communist China and still having relatives there did not seem to matter. Looking back, the attitude of the US Armed Services then could be described as homophobic. How times have changed for the better.

13

Ready to Step into the Unknown

I was reassigned to Hamilton Air Force Base in Marin County near the city of San Rafael. During the summer, I took a math course at San Francisco City College, and in the fall, I enrolled in two courses at East Contra Costa Community College. But shortly after midterm, the commanding officer transferred me to Parks Air Force Base, and I had to drop one course. For the basic algebra class, I was permitted to mail in my assignments and was given time off to take my final exam. During the spring term of 1958, I took two additional math classes at San Francisco City College. They were routine, and I don't remember much about them.

By this time I finally came to realize that it was unlikely I would get to go to Officer Candidate School and become a pilot. Thus, I decided to leave the Air Force. I was granted "early out"—ninety days before the four-year tour of duty was up—so I could start college in the fall.

Airmen who were mustering out were given a briefing about the benefits available to veterans. Two were of great interest to me: $300 in mustering-out pay and the educational benefits under the Korean War GI Bill that would enable me to go to college full-time. I learned that this assistance was provided both by the federal government and the State of California. These educational benefits were a "big bonus payout" and gave my life new direction.

I was instructed to check in at Travis Air Force Base halfway between San Francisco and Sacramento to receive my final discharge from the Air Force. Now as Airman First Class, one inch taller and twenty pounds heavier than when I enlisted, I had one remaining goal before checking out—I wanted to use three weeks of accumulated leave for one last trip to the Far East. I decided to take a gamble and hitchhike on military aircraft to visit my family and see Esther—I had not been able to forget her. I had often hitchhiked before, but not for such a long distance.

My first ride was on a cargo plane to Hickam Field, Hawaii. After a two-day layover, I caught a ride to Tokyo International Airport—which is now the downtown airport. There I found a pilot I knew for a hitch on a DC-3 to Clark Air Force Base.

My visit there was quite a letdown. The only people I recognized were the Filipino radio operators—most of the airmen I had known had left. When I went to see Esther's parents, they informed me she had moved to Manila and was engaged to be married soon to a Chinese businessman.

Two days later, I found a pilot willing to let me ride on his DC-3 cargo plane to Hong Kong.

Broadly smiling, my brothers and sisters chimed a welcome, "We're so glad to see you!"

My mother wanted to know, "Have you been reassigned to the Philippines?"

I explained, "No—I'm on my last leave. I'll soon be discharged from the Air Force."

With a frown, she asked, "What will happen to my getting the monthly allotment?"

I reassured her, "As soon as I start college, the allotment will continue under my GI Bill benefits. Also, I'm planning to work while attending college, so don't worry—I promise to keep sending you money."

Ready to Step into the Unknown

My time in Hong Kong was disappointing. Both Betty and Nonie had boyfriends. Thus every night I would go to a *mahjong* game and gamble till morning, then sleep most of the day. My mother was upset because I did not spend much time with the family. I did go to the US Consulate almost every day to work on the visa applications for my family to go to America. Father Des would continue to help with this process after I was no longer able to come to Hong Kong.

We (that is Chuck, Maria and I) already had money saved to pay for travel to the US for George and Milly who were to go and live with Maria and her husband Bob. The red tape was exacerbated because of the complicated status of the various family members still in Hong Kong: my mother was a Chinese citizen; George had US citizenship, but the other five children were stateless due to the Nationality Act of 1940.

Three days before my leave was to expire, I started to hitchhike back to the US. I caught a flight to the Philippines. There, I received a telegram stating, if I did not return to Travis Air Force Base in time, I would be considered AWOL. Within two days, I got to Japan, but then I was stuck. Day after day I tried but just could not find a flight back to the US. I did not have the funds for a commercial flight.

But while hanging around the flight line, I noticed at a far distance the takeoff and landing of a very strange-looking aircraft. The wingspan from tip to tip was longer than the fuselage. The wings drooped so much that people had to put wheels under the wingtips after the plane landed.

Finally, after five days, an air police captain asked, "Do you know how to use a .45 caliber pistol?"

"No, Sir. But I'm trained and qualified as sharpshooter

with a carbine."

Immediately, he handed me a .45 and showed me how to handle it. He chuckled, "Hold the pistol steady with both hands and keep it pointed away from your feet."

"Yes, Sir." I nodded to emphasize that I understood.

After this, the captain took me over to a cargo plane and ordered, "Stand guard until the pilot and crew show up."

The flight first took us to Wake Island, then to Hawaii. Each time we landed I had to stand guard while the crew took a break. I noticed that hundreds of film canisters were on board. Years later, when Gary Powers flying a U-2 was shot down by the Russians, I realized what I had seen were U-2s and what I had been guarding were classified films from secret U-2 flights.

I was five days late when I returned to Travis Air Force Base. Because I had notified them I would be delayed, I received nothing worse than a tongue-lashing from the sergeant in charge and was docked five days of pay.

The next day, on 15 August 1958, I was processed out of the Air Force, received my mustering-out pay and became a civilian again. I hitched a ride with an airman who was driving to San Francisco. My worldly possessions consisted of $300 plus small change in my pocket and a large duffle bag filled with military clothing and a few books. I closed my eyes as we left the base to avoid conversation.

Mentally, I reviewed the four years I had spent in the US Air Force. Although I did not achieve my dream of becoming a pilot, I learned to get along with people from all walks of life; I was trained to do a competent job; I found I could do well in college-level courses, and most importantly, I was able to provide for my family. I credited these achievements to my own efforts and good fortune—God was not in my

Ready to Step into the Unknown

life's frame of reference at this time.

Without a job, without a place to stay, without anyone who really cared about me, but with a head full of dreams and a heart full of hope—just like when I left Shanghai six years earlier—I brushed aside any doubt and feelings of apprehension. Instead, I resolutely set my mind on looking forward. For me, America now was a land with open opportunities to get more education as a path to position, recognition, wealth and freedom. I would shortly be 21, an adult by any account. I was ready to step into the unknown and continue my quest of becoming a true American—which no longer seemed to be far out of reach.

Epilog

Many years later, shortly before my retirement, I accepted an appointment as Distinguished Visiting Professor at the United States Air Force Academy in Colorado Springs. There I was teaching propulsion, engineering mechanics, and engineering design to cadets, many of whom would become pilots. The photo shows me in front of the chapel at the Academy in May 2011.

This job was my dream come true, but in a very different way than I had planned as a teenager. The path that God chose for me was indeed one that resulted in the greatest good overall. With my penchant for risk taking, I do not think I would have been a safe pilot. And I would not have met that frugal and charming exchange student who became my wife. But this is a story that will be in my next book.

In looking back to my childhood and youth, I would like to comment here about my experiences in two areas of danger to children and young people. My observations may help

Epilog

parents to protect their children from bullying and from sexual abusers.

Bullying seems to be a universal problem, even today. As a young boy, I was constantly bullied by Jackie Howard and his cohorts, and later on the ship by Kierkegaard Jørgensen. In both cases, I had no one to turn to. This has contributed to low self-confidence throughout my life. Also, I have not been able to help anyone else who faced this problem, including my children. I had serious problems with fear of rejection and failure. For example, after failing to become chancellor, I did not make any other serious attempts at a higher position above dean of engineering.

I wish I had had sufficient rapport with my children, so when they were bullied, they would have felt comfortable enough to discuss the situation with me and my wife. It took a while for us to recognize the problem with our youngest child, and in one case we transferred him to another school. Children should not have to solve the problem of being bullied on their own—which was the case both in my own as well as in my wife's childhood. But I have to confess that mostly my children were left to deal with the situation themselves.

The second problem—sexual abuse—is illustrated by my encounter with Horace. When I met Horace in the coffee shop at age 16, I immediately looked to him as this nice father figure wanting to extend a hand to me, a lonely stranger. I was naïve; I absolutely trusted that he was honorable and doing this because he was a kind and generous man. I did not suspect or understand that he was "grooming" me for sexual abuse.

Thinking in retrospect as an adult on this experience, I know that this is how sexual abuse of children often begins:

The potential predator befriends his or her victims, then grooms them—taking small steps in attempting to cross their boundaries—to see how far they can get. Even though I had traveled the world, in many ways I was still a kid at the time and alone. I can think about it rationally today, but it is even now very hard to talk about it. My description here has been toned down for younger readers (which makes it appear less serious than it was). Very often, abused children will be made to feel that the abuse was their fault. My father was very distant due to circumstances going back to war times, having had to leave China and his children, and his own lack of good parenting. Perhaps he may have been glad that Horace was ready to take care of me—I certainly accepted Horace as a father figure or friend whom I quickly got to know and trust. That I returned to him four years later for temporary shelter shows how strong that bond of friendship had grown during the time I was with him.

Both my wife and I grew up in a time and culture where sexual abuse was rarely acknowledged or talked about, to the point where we were naïve and oblivious that this could happen to our own children. My daughter recommends an organization called Kidpower as a resource. It teaches people how to set boundaries, to recognize when they are crossed, and how to keep themselves safe. It would be a comfort to me if my comments here could protect others from sexual abuse—that something good can come from the harm that I suffered. The worst lasting effect was not being able to build bonds of trust with other people and easily form close friendships throughout my adulthood.

About the Author

Edward Lumsdaine was born in Hong Kong and grew up in Shanghai, mostly during war times as told in his amazing story *Rotten Gambler Two Becomes a True American*. His mother was Chinese, his father an American merchant. After stints as a cabin boy and waiter on a Danish tramp steamer and four years in the US Air Force, he started college on the GI Bill at Ventura Junior College with little education past primary school. He met his wife-to-be (who was an exchange student from Switzerland) in English class. He then earned his BS, MS and PhD degrees in mechanical engineering, all at New Mexico State University.

After working for the Boeing Company as research engineer, his love for teaching combined with research lured him back to the academic life at South Dakota State, the University of Tennessee, and New Mexico State University. He advanced from Professor to administrative positions, including Dean of Engineering at the University of Michigan-Dearborn, the University of Toledo, and Michigan Technological University. In 2015, he and his wife celebrated their fifty-sixth anniversary. They have raised four children and built two passive solar homes. Later, they co-authored textbooks in engineering design and entrepreneurship that focus on creative problem solving. Also, together they have taught workshops all over the US and overseas. For more information, see www.InnovationToday.biz.

During a low period in his life, when he was struggling to overcome an addiction to casino gambling, he began to think about his roots in childhood and the struggles he faced in order to rise in his career. He found that writing memoir was very different from writing technical papers and engineering books. It was more like storytelling, and many people urged him to jot down what to them were almost incredible stories of survival.

For two years in a row, he attended the Blue Ridge Mountains Christian Writers Conference at the LifeWay Ridgecrest Center in North Carolina. The second year he submitted his book *You Bet Your Life* to the contest for unpublished writers and won third place for nonfiction. But the timing just wasn't right to publish it then, and the ending remained to be written. Also, the market was in a slump. Now, almost seven years later, he discovered an easy way to self-publish—through Amazon Kindle, starting with the story of his youth.

Since friends and family were asking for a softcover version, preferring to read from a book in hand, the Kindle manuscript was reformatted for this edition. Although the story is the same, the writing is not identical since it contains minor text editing, a few additional photos, and two maps, in an effort to achieve a quality page layout. Also running heads and page numbers had to be added.

Next in the works is the "love story" sequel, with the third and final part of Edward's life story to be tackled early next year. Now that he is fully retired, this project is surely a new adventure for him and his wife.

Made in the USA
Columbia, SC
10 July 2017